MW01256759

The Witches' Devil: Myth and Lore for Modern Cunning

ISBN 978-1-7367625-4-7
Moon Over the Mountain Press

The Witches' Devil

Myth and Lore
for Modern Cunning

Roger J. Horne

Contents

Figure I. A witch receives her mark and familiar. Adapted from *The History of Witches and Wizards* (1720).

Introduction

Now do we step into the dark. The lantern light flickers, its dim glow faltering even as you clutch it in your left hand tightly, the trail before us barely visible among the vines and weeds. The blackness of the woods at night surrounds us like a cloak. Crickets sound their trill. The cool air conjures clouds from our breath like a spell.

Somewhere in the distance, a voice enunciates some ancient speech we cannot quite make out, its echoes trailing high over the hills, its timbre wet-thick like the falling of branches after a storm. Perhaps it is not a voice at all. Perhaps it is merely the settling of the woods, a wind among the vines, some creature moving through the snarls of leaves and twigs.

Still, you cannot help but think it, and I cannot help but ask out loud: *Is it him? Is he here?*

Come with me, then. Let us walk, the two of us, and let us try to find him if we can. He is old now, older than he was when he taught the first witches at their fires, training them in arts so ancient the stones of the earth can't fathom. The ages of the world have changed him. Time has left him worn and thin and scattered, emerging in the old lore here and there as a whisper or a clue, hidden behind so many black doors we hesitate to open, mortal as we are.

But still, he lives. We witches feel his gaze when we are alone in the dark, our lips busied with the work of incantation. We hear him when the breeze whistles through an old oak tree. We feel his hands upon ours as we knot the cord, as we burn the herbs, as we place the pins of our age-old craft.

And for those who feel the call, we know that somehow, despite all of his flaws and all of his danger, he is ours—feared like us and maligned like us, alone like us, rebellious like us, hungry for knowledge like us, drawn to the dark like us, obedient to no lord like us, wild and longing to be free like us, forever an outsider and other, just like us. By some strange and ancient curse, the things we fear in him are most like us, imperfect and flawed, something godlike but unlike a god, a kindred and beloved whom we cannot touch to rescue, a mirror through which we cannot reach.

Let us go, then, in search of him. For fear of him, and for love of him.

Let us reach for the blackberry tucked just there, among the thorns, trusting that the sweetness we find will be worth the pricking of our thumbs.

Let us seek him out now. Let us haste and hurry to his call. Let no blind allegiance, no threat of Hell, no fear of shadows bar our way, for his prison is, in truth, our own. Along the winding trail we go now, you and I, to break the curse, to set each other free.

And, as the old lore says, "Devil take the hindmost, where 'er they be."

Figure 2. Witches work their waterside craft in the company of the Devil.
Adapted from *The History of Witches and Wizards* (1720).

Seeking the Witches' Devil

Witchcraft today enjoys a diversity and harmonious pluralism shared by few other spiritual traditions, a quality we should be eager to defend. However, for folk witches such as myself, whose arts are drawn from the lore and charm of previous ages, and for many other practitioners within the many-threaded tapestries of traditional craft, true progress in our art is hard-won and preciously rare, for a central jewel within the crown of our inheritance has been plucked out, excised as if by a surgeon's hand, cast out among the detritus, and many of us feel, from early on in our witchly studies, the ache of its absence, the feeling of something being missing that we cannot quite yet name.

For many of us, dear reader, that something is the witches' Devil. While the popular witchcraft of the midcentury won great gains in terms of establishing public acceptability, this reward came with a heavy price. This new witchcraft established an organized religion that was palatable and tolerable to those who previously despised us, stripped of the old lore pertaining to our Devil and the heretical, folk-religious cunning crafts, and while this new movement preserved within its folds many operative currents of old craft, it left others behind. This is not to minimize or denigrate the validity of Wiccan craft as it stands today, which is far richer and more diverse than what Gerald Gardner could have envisioned. Nor is it to suggest a lack of potency or completeness in the arts of our sister witches operating in this vein, for they are witness to their own deep mysteries and stand beside us as true kin. But we must recognize, painful as this truth may be, that in this reach for progress and unity, some of our treasures were left behind.

My own craft, like many folk witches practicing today, is shaped by my mixed heritage. I relish the old folklore of Scottish witchcraft and its smattering of early modern magics, particularly in the form of what we now call cunning craft, the folk rites and customs of everyday people who were poor in means but rich in lore. I treasure equally the folk charms and practical herbal knowledge of the Appalachian region in North America, which preserved many of the treasures brought over to these lands from Scotland. Some of my own direct ancestors were charmers and herb-doctors. Though they may have feared the Devil, they also preserved the many tales of him, told his stories around fires, and spoke his name, all while attending church, as was expected of everyone, and even adopting liturgical language into a blended body of heretical magics.

Claiming magical ancestry in modern times is so often viewed as mere posturing, but consider this: the lineage of folk witchery I describe is not as rare as one might think. Often, it is simply forgotten, abandoned by a daughter in the 1883 who became deeply religious and cast off the old superstitions of her mother, or shrugged off by a son in 1934 who left the farm for the university and thought his grandfather's remedies quaint and ignorant. If one goes back far enough, the roots of folk craft reach quite broadly. It is not only possible, dear reader, but entirely likely that you, yourself have something of a folk charmer somewhere in your ancestry. Even if you do not know or cannot say, for those ties are so often lost, you may share in that broader concept of spiritual ancestry among witch-kind, unbound by race or ethnicity, united in the milieu of cultures touched by diverse traditions of the old folk crafts. These currents are not closed, but open to all who belong to them, not dead, but vital, and their secrets are not bound by oaths and ceremonies, for they keep themselves, revealing truths and power when we prove ready to receive them. The openness of folk witchcraft is, in fact, central to its very nature, *folk* meaning *of the people.*

For many centuries, and for many generations, the lore of the Devil was widely, though fearfully, passed along. To describe this folkloric and mythic figure as merely the embodiment of evil is an oversimplification of his complex nature. He appears as the trickster on the spiritual journey, the deal-maker at the crossroads, the founder of the hosts of faery, the chief spirit of the magical grimoires, the soul within the vegetation of the land. He emerges as the serpent offering knowledge, the salmon of all wisdom, the beast of many coats and anatomies, the spirit of the wilderness. He boasts roles as rich and as varied as the angel of poisoning, the ruler of the dead, and the first sorcerer. Nor is he simply a male heteronormative figure; he morphs between male and female identities, his sexual appetites directed at all, a potent figure for queer and trans witches who are perhaps weary of the pseudo-historicism of gender essentialist concepts in modern witchcraft. Lastly, and perhaps most significantly, he is the instructor and initiator of witches, offering gifts of knowledge and power to those brave enough to seek him out in the darkness. In all of his forms, and in all of his lore, he offers powerful lessons of freedom and wisdom that can, if approached carefully, enrich our craft.

It is often presupposed, in discussions of the witches' Devil, that we are describing either a singular, ancient spirit who precedes human existence, who has always been and will always be, or a constructed image, a fabricated being invented by humans out of endlessly evolving cycles of myth and lore. From a modern animist perspective, though, both of these views are limited. The most powerful spirits, who are often conceived of as ancient ancestors, exist both within and through the practitioner. And our participation in the emergence and evolution of entities does not mean that the spirit is not real. Quite the contrary, it illustrates how and why the old lore matters, how it is our myths and legends that preserve and nourish the spirit's potency for future generations, that connect it to multitudes of human ancestors and adjacent cultures touched by the same currents of lore. This is how it is that so many folkloric texts (including the one you are reading now, dear reader) possess their own palpable magic, their own initiating spirit. The spirits of our old ones may incarnate and rebirth themselves by way of our words and symbols, but they are also real in themselves, for we witches can experience their presence intimately in our rites, and each new thread of lore we draw upon further vivifies and realizes this presence, sharpening our ability to perceive the otherworldly spirit incrementally, curtain after curtain being drawn back as we advance in our craft, until we are able to light our candle and see with our witch-sight at last those powers who have always stood beside us in the perfect dark.

And yet, the way to our Devil is obstructed by many dangers and anxieties. He is, after all, the king of Hell, appearing in the bible as both a tempter and a punishing angel. (Though, as we shall see, he is far more than a mere biblical figure.) We are told that he desires to possess us, to make us his own, to claim us forever for his dread kingdom. (His desire for us being, somehow, both frightening and confusingly erotic.) The Devil, we must admit from the very start, is not entirely benevolent. But then again, are we?

It is the tendency of all folk, both individually and collectively, to imagine ourselves decent. We paint the kindest pictures of ourselves, emphasizing our best qualities (or, more accurately, our most socially applauded qualities), while projecting those elements we despise in ourselves onto another, a scapegoat, in fact. On an internal level, we hide and shun those parts of ourselves we view as unacceptable, but in less symbolic terms, this projection is suffered by outcasts in society. Our culture ridicules the homeless, for their vulnerability reminds us of our fragile position within capitalism. We avoid the diseased, for they remind us that health is fleeting. We abandon the old, for we wish not to think on our own limited time here on earth. We ignore the voices of women, queer folk, and indigenous peoples, for we see and feel their undeniable suffering over the ages, and this reality challenges the justness of long-held systems of power. And not so many generations ago, our societies hung and burned witches, for they were guilty of possessing so many qualities our societies loathed: femaleness, knowledge, poverty, confidence, social oddness, imagination, ruralness, queerness, contrariness, and often enough, the talent for magic. The many trials of individuals sentenced for having performed simple folk magic using cords and poppets (charms that would have been well-known and used by many at the time) attest to this fact. Throughout our many ages, we have loathed different parts of ourselves in turn, justly or unjustly, and we have built the prison that holds our Devil in this way, brick by brick. But fear and anxiety are the thresholds of power, erected to hold us back from truths we are not yet sturdy enough to face. This is the curse we have wrought against ourselves: that as witches, some of our most potent secrets and magics are bound there, too. Our power and our Devil are locked up there together, and we cannot free the one without the other.

We must differentiate here between our approach to the Devil as folk and traditional witches and what has come to be called satanism. Most satanists today are atheists who view the Devil as simply a useful symbol for the political and societal "other"—the outcast or scapegoat. They do important work in the form of challenging the religious status quo and fighting for the rights of minorities, but their philosophy is largely humanist, and though folk and traditional witches may share in many of their political positions, satanists have virtually nothing to do with witchcraft.

Many witches today do, however, identify with the term *Luciferian*, which positions Lucifer as a being of enlightenment. Luciferianism on the whole, though, is largely theistic, and Luciferian organizations have traditionally regarded this being as a form of deity to be worshipped. Witches of the folk variety, like myself, can understand and sympathize with this position, but our engagement with our Devil is quite different in nature. The witches' Devil, for many of us, is spiritual, but not theistic. Our Devil is a teacher, not a god; an ancestor, not a deity; a figurehead of the otherworld, not an omnipotent presence. This is how it is possible for many a folk witch to attend church in the morning and call to the Devil at night, for our relationship with our Devil is not religious, but something else entirely, a belonging and kinship that binds us together, yet allows us to be free. If rejecting the Devil is the right-hand path, and worshipping him is the left-hand path, then the path tread by folk witches is a third way, another trail entirely, one that recognizes his presence as ally and even spiritual parent, but not quite master. This apparent contradiction has historically been difficult for outsiders to understand, but by looking to our lore and older myth, we come to see that syncretism and paradox are not problems to be resolved, but complexities to be embraced in the witches' craft, riddles and mysteries that reveal aspects of our Devil unique to the language of folk witchery.

Though the ultimate task of this book is to contribute to that slow and necessary unbinding of our Devil's (and, as witches, our own) potency, my intention is not to dictate to any witch the work of their own craft. Far from it; for witchcraft to be a living body of traditions and not a dead one, we must embrace fully and without reservation the many forms our traditions may take. Some traditions have never included the Devil at all, and for them, this absence is not a wound, but simply a continuation of who they are. We must acknowledge, too, that women have been subjugated and objectified by men for many centuries, and for many women, the idea of including the Devil in their craft simply feels like another man hoarding power. This is entirely valid, and though we will discuss lore that complicates the idea of the Devil as "male," there are too few spaces for women to exist without men, and this, too, like the curse that holds our Devil, is an imbalance that must be corrected. We must learn to look with love on our contradictions and divergences, appreciating difference as a form of strength, like a forest ecosystem inhabited by many kinds of beings, each with their own work to do in the world.

For my part, though, and perhaps for yours, dear reader, that work entails the healing of certain old curses, the correction of certain imbalances, and it is in this spirit that we must seek our Devil out at last. We shall avoid, to the best of our abilities, the temptation to dilute his potency into the broader categorical titles of "male polarity," "father god," or "horned god." Our subject is not so broad as this or so modern, but is quite simply the Devil himself as pertinent to witches. On the other hand, we shall also resist overstating his role as "master of evil," for that role has been played by many other spirits and deities over time, and lumping them all together does little to reveal his unique nature. Though this work of revealing must be tempered with well-sourced lore and myth, our larger goal is not historical, but spiritual: to sense out the lyrical truths distilled in our Devil. The balance of sourced fable and the spiritual reach for truth are like the clay vessel and the water held within; only with both can we bring back our cold drink from the well.

Perhaps, along the way, we can discover something about ourselves as folk and traditional witches, something true of our deep natures, an answer to the old questions of why we feel called to dark and forbidden places, why we are so contrary in our resistance to rules and definitions, why we harbor such strong distaste for authoritarianism, why we feel so called to support feminist work and to believe and trust in women, why we hate the vile crimes of the rich, why we simply cannot bring ourselves to throw out our traditions of cursing and hexing, why we hold knowledge itself to be sacred, why we find beauty and kinship in venomous creatures and poisonous flora that many would kill on sight, why we feel, in the company of the dead, some strange comfort, why forgotten tales and superstitions feel so much like old friends, and why we dare to call ourselves, despite the centuries of loathing and fear bound up in the term, *witches.*

Figure 3. The sorcerer conjures a demon. Adapted from *The Tragical History of the Life and Death of Doctor Faustus* (1620).

The Bound Spirit

Unlike the powerful entities recognized in other spiritual movements, the witches' Devil is not, in the strictest sense of the term, a god. He is not worshipped by most witches in the traditional way that one worships a deity, nor is he recognized as the creator of the universe. He does not hold unlimited power. He does not control the fabric of existence itself. He exists, by his very nature, on the periphery of things, and it is in this understanding that we find the true nature of his power. He is, much like his witches, a spiritual potency that many have tried to contain and subjugate over time, a captive of a condition he did not choose, a wild force, like the very soul of the witch, that others would like to see tamed, not only as a folkloric theme, but in actual magical acts aimed at controlling him. And yet, one of the deep mysteries of the witches' Devil is how his nature as a bound spirit does not weaken him, but instead seems only to increase his potency.

While most of us brought up today in Christian countries are familiar with the figure of the Devil from his biblical appearances, we must complicate this picture with folklore and fable in order to understand him fully as he pertains to witches. Let us begin, then, with a very straight-forward but interesting curse that appears in Scot's (1584) *Discoverie of Witchcraft*:

> I conjure thee Lucifer, with all thy soldiers, by the father, the son, and the Holie-ghost, with the humanitie and nativitie of Christ, with the virtue of all saints, that thou rest not day nor night, till thou bringest them to destruction, either by drowning or hanging, or that they be devoured by wild beasts, or burnt, or slaine by their enemies, or hated of all men living.

The Devil, as he appears here in his aspect as Lucifer, is not only available to the practitioner for cursing purposes, but is able to be subjugated and commanded to action. What this reveals about his nature and his history of engagement in human affairs and what this means for modern witches are complicated questions, and to arrive at the answers we seek, we will need to pick apart a few other connected threads of lore.

Of these, one of the most relevant pertains to the origination of the Devil's binding in Hell. The story of the fall of the proudest angel from his state of grace is a ubiquitous one, but a particularly striking passage can be found in the *Book of Enoch*, an ancient text estimated to be written sometime around two hundred B.C.E:

> And the Lord said to Raphael: Bind Azazel hand and foot, and cast him into the darkness: and make an opening in the desert, which is in Dudael, and cast him therein. And place upon him rough and jagged rocks, and cover him with darkness, and let him abide there forever, and cover his face that he may not see light.

Azazel is here given as the name of a leader among rebellious angels who defy the will of Heaven, and though the exact nature of his crime is an interesting point of discussion, we shall return to it later. For now, our focus is on the act of binding, on its long-reaching repercussions and magical echoes through the centuries, for this characterization of the Devil as a bound spirit has shaped much lore and magic over many ages, and without understanding its ramifications, we have little hope of accomplishing the task at hand and seeing our Devil rendered whole and visible at last.

This binding, as told in myth and lore, shaped many of the oldest concepts in operative occultism. In the pages of the *Grimorium Verum*, a sixteenth century grimoire of magical operations, we find three spirits listed as "superiors," denoting their rulership over the host of other entities described within this much-feared work: Lucifer, Beelzebuth, and Astaroth (Peterson, 2007).

Lucifer, we are told, appears to the magician as a handsome youth whose skin can be reddish in color. Beelzebuth adopts the form of a goat or calf. Astaroth lacks a gendered description here, but is described as being of both black and white coloration.

Figure 4. Sigil of Lucifer as provided in the *Grimorium Verum* (1700s).

Many have found this suggestive of the two halves of light and darkness, and also reminiscent of spiritual entities recognized as having both "white" and "black" aspects, such as the Puca Geal and Puca Dubh.

These three names and descriptions, though each distinct in origin, have all been used to describe our Devil over the centuries, and they are present in the wealth of other grimoires that echo this approach, including the similarly diabolical *Grand Grimoire*, which also includes Satanachia alongside the three already named. What matters most here, though, are two things: the positioning of the Devil as chief of spirits, who is understood as being locked away in the underworld of Hell, and the long pattern of magical operations designed to summon and constrain him and his ilk within a magical triangle or circle.

It is held as an unspoken truth behind the words of manuals in the grimoiric traditions that this being deserves his confinement to the abyss, and that the practitioner is just in threatening him, verbally berating him, and compelling him with sometimes violent magics to perform his will. In effect, the Devil is bound and harassed in order to achieve one's wish fulfillment, which is usually something less than noble: money, fame, the suffering of one's enemies, or even the ensnaring of some poor victim of the practitioner's non-consensual sexual appetites.

These grimoires, as disturbing as they may be to our modern sensibilities, contain a revealing tension. The practitioner seeks to wield the same forbidden arts for which these entities are supposedly damned. He imagines himself superior to them and calls upon the name of God and his angels in order to subjugate them, but ultimately, he only bothers with the operation because he desires the power these beings possess, because he values, in some way, their frightening natures, and he seeks to control them towards concrete ends in his own wish fulfillment. Though these texts contain some helpful formulae for the folk witch's repertoire, we tend to shun these passages as forms of spiritual violence. Still, it is not difficult to imagine the feeling of power one must have while attempting to summon and arrest the leader of the underworld's host. I imagine it must be similar to those who hunt lions for sport, who poach rare and endangered creatures for the rush of exhilaration they experience. It must be this, I think, or some other vile pleasure enjoyed by similar fools, many of whom end up on the wrong end of a horn.

Yet, the binding of mighty spirits in order to direct their power for one's own purposes is a practice far older than the 1500s. We find an account from the Greek Pausanias of an ancient binding of Enyalios, a god of war:

> Opposite this temple [of Poseidon] is an old image of Enyalius in fetters. The idea the Lacedaemonians express by this image is the same as the Athenians express by their Wingless Victory; the former think that Enyalius will never run away from them, being bound in fetters, while the Athenians think that Victory, having no wings, will always remain where she is. (Jones et al., 1918)

Similarly, though to different ends, we find descriptions in the work of Frazer (1890) of Roman legions calling to the tutelary god of the city they mean to conquer so that this spirit may be restrained safely outside the sphere of combat, now submissive to Rome and unable to aid its people in their moment of need.

Nor were these statues thought to be without pain as they lost their people. Corbeill (2009) notes the suffering expressed by an ancient statue of Apollo as preserved in the accounts of Augustine:

> Augustine presents a detailed critique of the
> tears produced by the statue of Apollo at
> Cumae during the second century B.C.
> Those tears, he maintains, provide clear
> evidence for the impotence of this and other
> pagan demons, since weeping demonstrates
> visibly that it lies outside the abilities of
> Apollo to guarantee either lasting peace or
> victory in war for his human worshippers.

Like these gods, our Devil is described in the
grimoiric tradition as subjugated in his fiery realm,
a power enslaved by both the god in Heaven and
the ceremonial magician on earth, an object to be
conquered rather than a subject in his own
narrative, a victim brutalized by other wills. It is
little wonder, then, that the grimoires describe
great dangers and the potential for madness and
death in the use of their operations. If we are fool
enough to go through with the thing, we will have
accomplished one of two ends: we have either
summoned a dangerous being who is incapable of
empathy and whose only desire is to spread
suffering itself, or we have unjustly offended an
ancient spirit whose nature lies outside of our

understanding, one who looks upon us as little more than a pest to be punished for this brief interruption of his mysterious work.

Nor can we overlook the long-lasting impact of Solomonic sorcery in terms of its tendency to confine and enslave so-called lesser spirits. Unlike the openly diabolical grimoires that conjure Lucifer, these works often purport to summon a host of djinn of various natures, each with a seal and name of their own, the most famous of these being the *Ars Goetia*. Despite *goetia* being commonly translated as "evil spirits," many of the beings described within this work are identified as friendly allies, able to impart knowledge of healing, settling strife between enemies, and understanding the natures of plants and stones. The word *goetia*, in fact, shares the root of *goeteia*, signifying witchcraft. Within this catalog of spirits, we find Berith, whose name is a barbarization of a god worshipped by the Canaanites, Flauros, whose name and sigil reveal roots in the Egyptian Horus, and Aamon, traceable to the pagan deity of Carthage, sharing the same root as the Egyptian Amun-Ra. As Margaret Murray famously wrote, "the God of the old religion becomes the Devil of the new." She was quite right, it turns out, though she erred in imagining a singular, monolithic Devil rather than a diverse and pluralistic host of beings, much as she mistakenly imagined a paradigmatic historical priesthood of witches instead of the wide variety of very real cunning traditions that make up the lineage of actual witches.

In terms of practical contact with our Devil in his many iterations, an important question now presents itself. If the spirit catalogs in the grimoires were written secretly by priests and monks within the church, a fact on which most scholars agree, then what are we witches to make of the subjugation of these ancient spirits, now reduced so small as to fit ten to a page, stripped of their peoples and their temples? And how will we be received when we call upon them using the instruments and designs of their enemies, by those who would attempt to torment them and bind them ruthlessly for petty gains? Will they recognize us as kin, or will they mistake us for their old abusive "masters" of previous centuries?

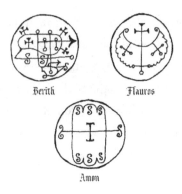

Figure 5. Goetic sigils for Berith, Flauros, and Amon.

A partial answer to this question lies in the ways witch-lore differs from the Solomonic manuals in terms of the methodology of spirit conjuration. While the grimoire tradition speaks of elaborate rituals and constraints placed upon the spirit, witch-lore speaks of far simpler and less aggressive means for permitting the spirit to make contact.

Alexander Hamilton, an accused Scottish warlock in the 17th century (not the American historical figure), was said to strike thrice upon the ground in order to call the Devil (Murray, 1931). Agnes Sampson, a healer and accused witch in 16th century Scotland, was said to use the words "Elva, come to me" in order to call to the Devil, either in his own form or in the form of her familiar. Another Scottish practitioner named Andro Man was said in the late 1500s to call the Devil with the word "Benedicite" and to bid him farewell again with "Maikpeblis." In 1629 in Orkney, Jonet Rendall was accused of calling the Devil with the name "Walliman." Swedish witches in 1670 were claimed to have called out "Antecessor, come and carry us." The infamous Somerset witches of 1664 were said to simply cry out the name "Robin," a reference to the friendlier, folk-given name of "Robin Goodfellow."

These forms of spirit conjuration, which are themselves a kind of unbinding, make use of a variety of names, and their simple rituals feel more personal, even improvisational. In these differences we recognize two truths. The first is that witches practicing in folk tradition have less need of the elaborate bells and whistles found in the ceremonial traditions; we are calling not to an enemy, but to a beloved, to our own kin. For us as modern folk and traditional witches, the magical formulae for forging the necessary connection with this spirit are more ecstatic than ceremonial, achieved through a bending of consciousness through substance use, repetitive rhythmic activities, and visionary states in order to achieve a personalized experience of spirit presence.

The second truth here is that the Devil is, in fact, a pluralistic being containing multitudes. Not only do witches, even those of us practicing today, have personal, secret names for our Devil, but we also recognize the plethora of "demonic" names noted in grimoires as minor aspects of his being—pieces, in fact, of his whole. That our Devil is identified in some grimoires as the emperor over these spirits is merely another way of saying that his presence reaches out and through these more specific facets of spirit form, like the roots of a tree that split and fragment in so many directions, weaving their way through the soil. Perhaps this is why the accused Alsace witch Anna Wickensipfel, in 1586, was said to simply call out "in the name of a thousand devils."

One wonders about the connection between the ancient practice of binding gods and the early modern practice of magically restraining the kings of Hell. On the one hand, we have the ancient Romans, chaining and magically binding the gods of their enemies in order to prevent them from saving their people from imperialization. On the other, we have priests and monks of the Roman Catholic Church, whom historians believe to have authored so many of the grimoires centuries later, binding and cataloging their demons, who are in truth the old pagan gods of conquered peoples, recast with new (though still identifiable) names. It is as if the spiritual violence of imperialization cannot halt its momentum, a phantom desiring to consume everything to its benefit, unable to stop even after its empire is long gone.

I do not mean to suggest here the literal oppression of an ancient, unified cult devoted to the Devil. This is the stuff of fantasy and the romanticization of witchcraft, which has left many folk witches with very real and tangible folk magical heritage confused, operating under the mistaken impression that, since their ancestors were not robe-wearing priests in some ancient, dogmatic cult of the Old One, their inherited folk magics must not be as legitimate. The awakening taking place now among folk and traditional witches reveals that this is nonsense. Witchcraft is not and has never been a unified, singular tradition, nor has our Devil ever been contained within the imagery of only one culture, instead arising from diversity and syncretism, from the cracks between dogmas and folkloric currents of understanding. Like witches, the Devil resists being stamped out because of his slippery nature, being a bit of this and a bit of that. The modern urge to create dogma and elitism within witchcraft—the invention of long-winded titles, the imaginary "degrees," the self-appointed "magisters" proclaiming their one-size-fits-all models of craft—all of these machinations do little more than bind us in new ways. As we bind the spirit, so do we bind ourselves. Perhaps the larger point here is that, given the history of the binding of pagan gods, we should consider carefully what this spiritual violence accomplishes, how it changes the nature of the spirit being bound, how it changes us on an internal level, and why, perhaps, we might go about the process of magical mastery in another way that draws power from freedom instead of imprisonment, from release instead of binding, from permission instead of restraint, disrupting this pattern of spirit aggression and self-aggression through the ages.

The tale of "Stingy Jack," a popular bit of folklore surviving to this day, echoes these themes of binding in a way widely recognizable to our ancestors. There exists no shortage of folklore in which the Devil is tricked or trapped in order to thwart his efforts and accomplish some form of gain on behalf of the protagonist. In this particular story, Jack tricks the Devil into taking the form of a small coin, which he then places inside his wallet, sealing him inside, unable to escape. Upon Jack's death, he is then told that he is unwelcome in Hell. Being also unfit for Heaven, his spirit is fated to wander the earth until judgment day. It is interesting that Jack's fate in this story is cast as more pitiable even than those in Hell, that in trapping the Devil, who is certainly a dark trickster in this tale, he has committed some manner of sin that must be punished in the course of the narrative.

One cannot help but see similarities in this story to the old folktale of the soldier who traps death. Having been gifted with a magical sack that seals away anyone who is commanded to go inside it, the soldier first practices the trick on a group of devils, finding it effective. "Get in," he says, and so they are sucked into the magical sack. He later decides to confine death himself by the same means. Realizing that death is the end of suffering and not its cause, he releases him, but like Jack, he is found unfit for Heaven or Hell, and so he is doomed to wander, deathless and alone, unable to find rest, punished for abusing power in order to restrain forces that, though dark and fearsome, are part of the necessary balance of the world.

Interestingly, we see in the figure of the Devil some old vestiges of ancient pagan gods of the underworld, those keepers of the dark abodes of the dead. This makes sense, for if the mythic and grimoiric traditions speak of the Devil as an imprisoned being, he must have a vast and worthy prison indeed. His pitchfork, an accessory now ubiquitous in the Devil's iconography, finds its ancient roots in Hades, the Greek god of the dead, who wielded the bident, a stick with two prongs that bears much resemblance to the forked branches and stangs employed by modern folk and traditional witches in our arts. This two-pronged tool of art notably appears throughout folk-magical sources, notably in the European *Grand Grimoire* as a "blasting rod" used for magical ends, and again in the new world as the forked branch noted in Appalachian folk magics in order to draw a circle (Thomas & Thomas, 1920). The branch given in this source is made of willow, long known for its associations with passage to the underworld.

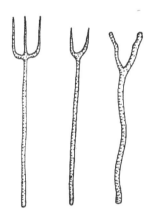

Figure 6. The trident, or Devil's pitchfork, alongside the bident and stang, blasting rod, or forked branch.

If our Devil does indeed retain an aspect as lord of the dead, this explains why his demons, as they appear in the old grimoires, are so often commanded to conjure the spirits of the deceased. Among the goetia, Bifrons (meaning "two-faced," a not insignificant detail that connects this being with the old god Janus and with our very Devil) is suggested to assist with workings of necromancy in that he "changeth Dead Bodies, and putteth them in another place; also he lighteth seeming Candles upon the Graves of the Dead." In the *Grimorium Verum*, the spirit Frucissiere is also described as having power over the dead. We must, of course, read these descriptions with an eye for poetry, as the visionary experience of spirits, usually conducted in an altered state of consciousness, can differ from one practitioner to another, and the imagery here of lighting candles on graves may have a few different meanings.

The term *necromancy* was commonly used in the early modern period as a way of categorizing dark sorcery in general (despite the fact that its trappings are today understood as much more specific) that it was used against all manner of charmers, conversation with the spirits of the dead being thoroughly associated with witchcraft itself. However, unlike the workings of witches, necromancers were understood to utilize biblical passages and names of God in their art in order to compel these spirits to arise, often with the aid of some enslaved spirit or another from the grimoires. It seems even the dead could not rest without being bound and commanded in the same manner as our Devil.

Nor is the Devil without familial bonds in his pit. In the folktale of the three golden hairs, we see that the Devil is said to dwell in Hell with his grandmother.

Figure 7. Circle for raising the spirit Oberion. Adapted from
The Astrologer of the Nineteenth Century (1825).

Tasked with acquiring three golden hairs from the Devil himself, a boy ventures into the underworld, enduring many tests and trials, but it is through the efforts of the Devil's grandmother that the boy survives and succeeds in his quest. We see her feed the Devil, soothe him to sleep, and hold his head in her lap. Early publications of this story found the idea of the Devil possessing family so strangely sympathetic that they simply edited him into a "giant" rather than the Devil. Along similar lines, the common expression of "the Devil's wife" is suggestive of some hellish company. Folklore is not fiction, though; it is the lore of the people, arising from shared, communal tales passed along over time, and so it seems the people of previous ages themselves found it difficult to imagine the Devil being bound in Hell without some companionship.

We even see, in Leland's (1899) very famous folkloric compendium, *Aradia,* a mention of a magical practitioner binding and threatening the spirit of Diana, daughter of the first witch by way of Lucifer:

> I do not bake the bread, nor with it salt,
> Nor do I cook the honey with the wine;
> I bake the body and the blood and soul,
> The soul of great Diana, that she shall
> Know neither rest nor peace, and ever be
> In cruel suffering till she will grant
> What I request, what I do most desire...

Is the spirit of Diana, as presented in this passage, queen or servant? The energy of these words lies in the command of a powerful force, positioning the charmer, for a moment, as her superior. But power is slippery and does not like to be held forever, and one wonders how Diana will approach the offender later, when they are without it. Leland notes this interesting passage as evidence of a violent trend, comparing it to the threatening of images of the saints in similar folk charms in order to procure a favor. As we have seen, the trend is wider even than that, so large that even the goddess of the moon herself has perhaps had to put up with would-be abusers.

Spiritual memories echo across myth and lore in so many iterations, repeating themselves in new contexts until we are able to master the lesson. Perhaps this is why we see the similar treatment of ensnarement, imprisonment, and binding applied to mortal witches in many currents of lore. Davies' (1975) *The Silver Bullet*, which have become an important text in Appalachian spheres of witchery, recounts tales of witches restrained and distracted by the task of counting, one Virginia tale in particular noting that the spirits of witches, when traveling about at night, must stop and count every hole in a sieve, every piece of gravel before a doorstep, or otherwise commit to some act of tedium set before them, trapping them in a passive and arrested state until morning comes. Similarly, the witch's spirit may be entangled in its own magics by burning, beating, or otherwise enacting violence upon some object touched by the witch or crafted to look like them, effectively capturing the spirit in an object to act as magical simulacrum. It is known and understood that folk charmers of various ilk used charms like these to arrest the efforts of practitioners who were perceived to be dangerous, but if charms as violent as these were used, how different can we really say these "white witches" were from the so-called "black witches" or malevolent witches? We witches are, it seems, expected to suffer the same rules of entrapment and humiliation as our Devil and the host of spirits associated with him in the old grimoires. Or perhaps not.

Perhaps, if time and experience are our teachers, we may still heed the lesson. By removing (with great care) the bindings placed by others upon the potent spirits with whom we partner, perhaps we can achieve some manner of freedom ourselves, untying the rope that restrains those parts of our spirit that we may call our dark selves, our deep selves, the half of our soul that lies in the otherworld, a part that, as we shall see, is kin to our Devil and to his host of spirits in more ways than one.

In practical application, this art most famously takes the form of the witch's tradition of speaking the lord's prayer backwards. Like the disappearing lexical charms of ABAXACATABAX and ABRAHADABRA, the intention in pronouncing this prayer backwards is a form of undoing, a charm of release.

Huson (1970) even goes one step further than the old lore, suggesting that the witch utilize their spiritual perception to "see" chains and cuffs crumbling away from their body. Often given as a kind of prayer to the Devil, the charm becomes, in this context, a method for unbinding of the witch's soul from the long history of magical operation aimed at restraining and subjugating the sacred dark. We are, in effect, unspeaking the many layers of binding and entrapment laid over the centuries.

More importantly, though, we can employ this wisdom to guide our interactions with familiar spirits, ancestral spirits, and yes, the beings that have been called demons. What I suggest is not that we imagine all spirits friendly and harmless, for that is simply foolishness, but that we perhaps adopt the same perspective we might use when dealing with strangers in our daily lives. I have offered in other books the metaphor of the visitor at the door, and it bears repeating here. Would we greet a stranger knocking upon our door with a blowtorch, or would we try to understand first who they are, what they want, and why they are here before we proceed to make a new enemy?

This does not mean abandoning our charms of protection, our trusted ancestors and familiars who act as sentinels at our threshold. It does not mean inviting strange spirits into our homes and our lives before testing them and slowly building trust over time. What it does mean is acting with the same kindness in the spiritual world as we expect in the physical one, to consider that they have as much right to exist as we do, to inspect carefully our assumptions about spirits based on what may be biased accounts, perhaps relying on divination practices in order to better understand their natures rather than assaulting every spirit around us with broad and ham-fisted exorcisms. And most importantly, if we expect to nourish the spirit of freedom within ourselves, our practices can never include enslaving another sentient being to our wills.

We may even encounter, in the course of our work in our craft, spirits who suffer bindings applied by the fools of previous generations. Again, we must proceed with great care, for even a gentle creature, when frightened, will try to bite the hand that reaches to free it from the trap. These beings, regardless of their bindings, are still potent and strong, but they are not, in my experience, immune to suffering. Worse still, dark entities do not simply endure suffering kindly by turning the other cheek, but become enraged, venomous, and vengeful over time, suspicious of modern humans, having been exposed to endless generations of barbaric treatment.

The building of trust with dark entities is a dangerous matter, and it is one that takes a long time, but it can still be accomplished if we remember that darkness and evil are distinct concepts often misconstrued, that creatures who favor the dark (ourselves as witches included) seek after its serenity and restoration, its respite from the glaring and intrusive light of day, like the toad that prefers the cool night, knowing that its soft body is vulnerable to predators in the harsh sun. We must respect the bound spirit's privacy and agency, building our relationship with measured, slow, confident steps. We must allow it to retain its mystery. We must accept that we are not entitled to its treasures, its secrets, its deep truths simply because we have some magical talent. We must somehow learn, like our kin in the otherworld, to relish the freedom of the dark and to swim in its mystery, to release our need to see everything, to scrutinize, study, and catalog it all in a doomed effort to somehow own it all, to make of the world, in fact, an empire.

Figure 8. Horned spirit. Adapted from *Robin Goodfellow, His Mad Pranckes and Merry Jests* (1628).

Light Between the Horns

Though often associated with darkness, the witches' Devil is also, as evidenced in myth and lore, a being of light. He is the candle set between the horns, the star heralding the dawn, the shining constellation of Heaven's bull. He is the bonfire of May Eve, the blessing of the candles in folk custom, the leap of flame from one wick to another. He is the luminous body that is female and male, risen and fallen, the figure beset with the crackling fire's glow—and the long shadow cast in its wake.

The depiction of the witches' sabbat preserved in Heinrich Heine's (1892) *Faust* is notable for its inclusion of a specific detail of diabolical lore that is very often overlooked, but crucial for this exploration of the witches' Devil as a luminous being. In this passage, drawing on well-established witch-lore, he describes the sabbat meeting-place:

> A broad plain on the summit of a mountain. Trees on either side, on whose branches hang strangely formed lamps, which illuminate the scene. In the midst is a stone pedestal or block, like an altar, on which stands a black goat with a black human face, and a burning candle between the horns...Before the goat's altar a man and woman walk up and down, each bearing a black candle; they bow before the back-side of the goat, kneel down, and pay it the homage of a kiss. Meanwhile new guests come riding through the air on brooms, pitchforks, great spoons, or on wolves and cats.

How detailed and glorious is this depiction captured in Heine's play? Although we might spend a great deal of time unpacking so many elements here, what deserves the most attention for our purposes now is the inclusion of the "burning candle between the horns." This figure captures a potent and enduring symbol that is preserved in so many currents of lore.

In modern practice, witches operating in folk and traditional currents often associate the "light between the horns" with the fire of cunning, a symbol of the power and wisdom passed along to the new witch by the Devil (or sometimes by a figure identified more ambiguously as "witch-father"). This fire is seen as illuminating, allowing us to perceive in ways we did not before advancing in our craft, but it is also transformative, in that fire consumes and transforms, gifting prehistoric humanity with the craft necessary to create heat, safe food, medicine, and metals.

This passing of the fire from the source to the individual is a pattern evidenced throughout old lore and charm. We see it present in older traditions of the Beltane fire or May Eve fire, which emphasize the communal effort of the bonfire and the blessing it bestows upon the community:

> The night before, all the fires in the country were carefully extinguished, and the next morning the materials for exciting this sacred fire were prepared. The most primitive method seems to be that which was used in the islands of Skye, Mull, and Tiree...The

> fire had the appearance of being immediately
> derived from heaven, and manifold were the
> virtues ascribed to it. They esteemed it
> preservative against witch-craft, and a
> sovereign remedy against malignant diseases,
> both in the human species and in cattle; and
> by it the strongest poisons were supposed to
> have their nature changed. (Frazer, 1890)

We must remember that many of the old cunning charms were utilized "against witchcraft"; though ironic, this reinterpretation of "craft against craft" was useful for establishing the roles of healers and cunning folk in communities. It also helped many (though not all) avoid the noose. The fact that all the fires in the country were extinguished before the lighting of the Beltane fire seems a passing detail in this passage, but it is also important, since this fire would be used to light torches and lanterns that may be carried back to each home, thereby the single ritual fire lights, heats, and empowers each individual house, and the fire is "passed" in a quite literal way across the community.

We see this passing of the fire, too, in the surviving traditions of Candlemas, which is the origin of the American Groundhog Day (originally associated more closely with the serpent, though still a propitious day to foretell the length of winter). This date is associated with both witch-lore and Devil-lore. Witches at Auldearne in the early modern period were believed to conduct rites at this time, the following account being one particularly strange and vivid example:

> Before Candlemas we went be-east Kinloss, and there we yoked a plough of toads. The Devil held the plough, and John Young, our Officer, did drive the plough. Toads did draw the plough as oxen, couch-grass was the harness and trace-chains, a gelded animal's horn was the coulter, and a piece of a gelded animal's horn was the sock. (Murray, 1931)

The mass of the candles conducted on this date, which involves blessing the candles to be used in the church throughout the coming year, can be traced as far back as 400-500 C.E., but even in that age it appears to have been known already. It has been suggested to find its origins in older traditions of the pagan Lupercalia, adopted and spread by the Roman Catholic Church across the

western world. It is common in this public ritual
for candles to be brought from parishioners to be
blessed for home use, and this practice ingrained
itself in so many currents of old folk magic and
cunning craft that modern folk witches hold it dear
to this day. Once again, we see heretical deviations
of church-spread symbols that, ironically, have
pagan origins, transformed by the church and then
reintroduced to new pagans and adapted again, our
wise ancestors seeing within these rituals the
vestiges of potent charm and craft.

These ancient echoes of past symbolism are
sometimes surprising. The candle between the
horns of our Devil has, in fact, a very visible
connection with the figure of the Baphomet. This
image, which was believed at one time to have
been worshipped in Freemason temples, is perhaps
a case of syncretic myth made whole and newly
incarnate. The image with which we are familiar
today, thanks to the work of French occultist
Eliphas Levi, is a humanoid figure with the head
of a goat, who bears a torch positioned between
its two horns. Christoph Friedrich Nicolai, in
1782, suggested that the name *Baphomet* would
have come from the Greek *baphe metous*,

meaning "baptism of wisdom." Regardless of this figure's syncretic origins, it quickly permeated early modern lore and flavored many of our most popular images of the Devil, contributing to the milieu of his personality, now emphasizing his role as the holder of some form of spiritual fire, the keeper of some ancient torch, positioned between two horns. Even more interesting is this figure's combination of male and female anatomy, having a suggested phallus in the form of a caduceus, but also very clearly having breasts. This is only further evidence of this figure's syncretic nature, drawing from both male and female mythic figures.

This image, though cemented by Levi, would not have been invented in its entirety in western Europe, for we know that it echoes older pagan themes found further east. The "bull of Heaven," which appears in the *Epic of Gilgamesh*, is associated with Ishtar (Inanna to the Sumerians), and it has long been suggested to have its origins in the constellation of Taurus. Ishtar, as a star goddess, was even later syncretized with mythologies of Epona and depicted as riding her great bull. We have here, in effect, a star resting atop a horned beast.

Figure 9. Baphomet. Adapted from *La Magie Noire* (1800s).

Isis, too, in Egyptian imagery, is depicted with the horns of a bull and a light that appears to be a solar disk positioned between them. In these figures, we see ancient echoes of the light between the horns, here expressed as a goddess who is the star between the horns.

If our leap between Ishtar and Baphomet seems difficult to make, we have only to look at the old grimoires known to our cunning craft ancestors for the missing piece, for we see there the remains of Ishtar, who, having been syncretized with the similarly named Astarte, is presented to us transformed as the demonic power named Astaroth in multiple early modern manuals of magic.

Figure 10. Seal of Astaroth from the *Ars Goetia.*

In the *Ars Goetia*, even the seal given here for this being utilizes the pentagram or star form, an old remnant of her origins as a star goddess and yet another echo of this ancient light between the horns. Our "witch-father," it seems, who passes unto us his flame of cunning in his generously offered baptism of wisdom, is not entirely father, but also mother, revealed as a syncretic spirit informed by both male and female identities.

It is far too common for modern pagans to conflate syncretism with reductive views of deity. In the ancient world, the syncretism of deity was actually very common. These long-lost cultures did not sit in one place, but traveled, traded, and communicated, and as they did so, they noticed similarities between and among their gods, resulting in blended spirit identities that evolved quite naturally and made perfect sense to them. This is why we see in mythology and ancient magical manuals deities like Hekate-Ereshkigal and Dionysus-Osiris. In modern practice, we witches view similar connections between ancient figures, but here we must be careful. Reduction happens when we align our syncretisms with purely modern concepts or ideas that are too wide and all-encompassing to mean anything, which has often been done by reducing all goddesses into one goddess or all gods into one god. If all these figures have in common is maleness or femaleness, how do we begin to understand the threads that connect them? What, then, is their nature?

The trap in the reduction of deity by gender is this: we enshrine our modern socially constructed gender roles as sacred and ancient, which should make us uncomfortable for many reasons. This sanctification of modern gender roles expresses itself as a supposed "sacred calling" of men to be hunters, warriors, providers, and fathers, all of these things being enshrined in modern masculinity. We exclude the intellectualism, creativity, and homoeroticism that characterizes many ancient forms of masculinity because these things are less palatable in our modern heteronormative societies. Similarly, women are suddenly charged with a variety of "sacred" roles in the name of some vast and nameless "goddess": motherhood, nurturing, virginity, domesticity, gentleness, beauty. We often exclude from this paradigm qualities of ferocity, leadership, and innovation—those female warriors, leaders, poets, and artists who did, in fact, exist in ancient times— because they do not fit modern concepts of femininity. Women, we should know by now, are more than this. These gender-based reductions are harmful, for they leave many pagans feeling unwelcome in our traditions, but they are also simply not historical.

In understanding our Devil through his syncretic origins, though, our story is made richer and more complex rather than suffering reduction. His candle is starlight, his breasts are those of the old pagan goddesses, his horns are both the beast-gods of the ancient world and the horned headdress that is the crescent moon itself, as in the famous Hillah statuette of Ishtar. His "baptism of wisdom" is our state of being bathed in light, the light of illumination and the literal light of our altar candles and bonfires. We do, in fact, carry this fire, in the sense that a torch is carried, through generations of magic and craft, preserving the wisdom we earn in the form of lore and charm, drawing our source from those candles passed our way from the sorcerers of previous ages who tended such sacred fire, preserving it in our lore.

We are not finished hunting down this aspect of our Devil, however, because there remains more to glean from the significance of the pentagram-as-star in his imagery. Similar to the seal of Astaroth as provided in the *Ars Goetia*, we find in the pages of the fourteenth century grimoire known as the *Clavicula Salomonis* a seal provided for the spirits of Venus, and it takes a discernably similar shape:

Figure 11. Simplified form of the Second Pentacle of Venus
from the *Clavicula Salomonis.*

While modern traditions of witchcraft often use
the pentacle (usually with modern associations of
five elements, senses, fingers on the hand, etc.),
this symbol is actually not all that common in
older sources compared to triangles, hexagrams,
and squares, which are much more numerous in
the grimoires, and so it stands out here among
the many other glyphs. This seal, provided as the
"Second Pentacle of Venus," echoes the
pentagram form we see in the seal of Astaroth,
and perhaps not without reason.

Venus is, most certainly, a very visible star in
our night sky, but the pentagram is not the only
shape used to convey a bright star, so we may
wonder why this specific geometrical form feels so
meaningful and correct here in the *Clavicula
Salomonis.* Another convergence makes this

connection clear, though, and that is the lines created when one traces the movements of the planet Venus from a perspective that places earth at the center of the image, in line with ancient thinking about the universe. Ancient cultures were quite sophisticated in tracking the movements of stars, and their astrologers were most likely well aware of this pattern. By the 1300s, when the *Clavicula Salomonis* was most likely written, this pattern would certainly have been known. But if the pentagram is emblematic of the star of Venus, it is also suggestive of the morning star, for they are one and the same. The morning star, of course, appears in the bible as *Lucifer*, indicating both the star of Venus and the "light-bringing" morning star spirit associated with that name.

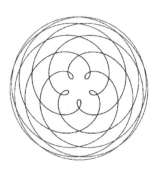

Figure 12. Illustration of the geocentric orbit of Venus.

This figure is rooted in the Greco-Roman spirit personified under various names, including the similar-sounding *Phosphorus.*

Ancient names are often misleading, but in this case, there seems to be some mythological commonality between Lucifer as fallen angel and ancient pagan deities for the morning star. Day (2010) discusses how the Canaanite deity Atta (a male form of Ishtar) attempted to overthrow the higher god Ba'al, and being defeated, fell from the heavens into the underworld. This tale, it seems, was meant to convey and connect with the rise and fall of the morning star, which is chased away by the sun. Similarly, we can read the descent of Inanna, an ancient Sumerian myth of another deific sojourn into the underworld, as a female iteration of this tale, conveying the same mythic themes and spiritual symbols.

And so, it seems that our star in the form of a pentagram *does* have something to do with our Devil after all, though perhaps not in the manner we would have imagined based on modern depictions. And our fire, it seems, which graces the altars of so many modern witches, holds a continuity in the lore that retains its potency. But what are we to make of the aggregate nature of these aspects of our Devil, being sourced not in one place or culture, but in many, arising out of so much spiritual discourse and convergence over so many centuries?

When fire is passed from one candle to another by lighting the new wick, it is both a continuity and a departure into something new. It is not, we know, the same fire, since fire is not a substance that can be passed but a process of burning, a light that leaps between. Perhaps we can view ourselves, as modern practitioners, in this manner, as both the descendants of our Old One who is the Devil, carrying that fire forth on our own candles, and a new people living in a different age. The old lore matters, and the old words matter, but what matters most is their *spirit*, their fire, an immaterial thing that cannot be passed to us directly in the manner of an inheritance, but must be awakened within us.

We might also consider the complex presence of gender in this aspect of our Devil, which lives on even in the Marseille tarot illustration of the Devil from the 1600s, complete with breasts.

Figure 13. The Devil of the Marseille Tarot trump sequence (1700s).

In his ability to encompass maleness, femaleness, and many things both and neither, we are challenged as practitioners of the craft to view ourselves along less rigid terms. Modern notions of balance between "male and female energies" fall short of this endeavor. Our Devil's gender does not embody a schism or a dualistic nature. His maleness and femaleness neither conflict with one another nor complement one another. Rather, he simply is. His synergies have evolved organically along the lines of connected symbol and meaning. His gender is a complex reality that simply does not fit, by any reckoning, into modern heteronormative models, and if this makes us uncomfortable as witches, all the better, for the otherness he embodies is a potency that is not tapped without discomfort.

The challenge our Devil offers also clashes against patriarchy itself. We see how female deities from previous ages became compounded in this imagery, resigned to the abyss in the cosmology of Christianity in the wake of its growth and spread across the western world. The femaleness in the Devil's symbolism is no mere accident, and it is also no accident that most of his initiates in early modern witch-lore are women. In a world in which no major religions hold space for female power, in a culture that hates and maligns women, that stands by rapists and abusers while ignoring the culture that creates them, feminine bodies and feminine qualities are ostracized to the margins of spirituality. And yet, they do not disappear, but persist. In our Devil, the self-loathing many women are taught is transformed, for we see in the imagery of the Devil those elements of femaleness itself, and if such a potent spirit can be female, we are called to uproot our own misogyny. In the poetic mythos of Hell, we can imagine that the sacred feminine carves out its own space and takes its own rightful power, not by appealing to and appeasing the misogynistic dominant culture and its patriarchal notions of fathers, sons, and salvation, but by rejecting these entirely, turning instead to the light of illumination within the abyss that is, in fact, the star of Astaroth.

In broader strokes, the symbol of the light between the horns captures the love of all knowledge, even forbidden knowledge, shared amongst witches. We are told in so many terms that ignorance is bliss, that we should strive to be like children, but for so many of us, these efforts do nothing to quench the thirst that compels us to seek out our truths. While the light of the sun is a light we cannot control or direct, leaving many places of shadow across the landscape, the light of the candle or torch is ours to wield. We carry it with us into places of darkness, discerning for ourselves what is for us and what is not. It is our own sun, wielded by our own hand, and though it will not dispel the darkness of night that certainly enshrouds many dangers, it offers freedom and autonomy, the ability to choose for ourselves. One cannot help but imagine the first humans to wield fire, to realize that this primal force of nature can be directed and used to see, to warm, and to craft. We witches are like these early fire-wielders, able to see in the night-time forest for the first time, empowered with light, but also overcome with wonder.

Figure 14. Witches convene with the Man in Black in a woodland scene.
Adapted from *The History of Witches and Wizards* (1720).

Spirit in the Green

The natural world—sometimes referred to now as the "green" world—is in fact, quite simply, the world. Modern celebrations of "nature" are decidedly romantic, even among witches, focusing on aesthetic beauty while ignoring the important roles of non-ornamental plant life (which is to say not considered beautiful, but very often useful) and the demanding, often ugly details of sowing and harvesting food and medicine, removed as we are from that labor. But in older generations, this was not always so, and the old charmers and tale-tellers saw the Devil's handiwork often in the forests and fields. The seasonal cycles of death and rebirth heralded very tangible comforts and discomforts that would have been meaningful in daily life. Let us embark by plumbing the symbol of the tree as a spiritual fulcrum point uniting the lore of pagan spirits, faeries, witches, and the Devil together. Folkard's (1884) *Plant Lore, Legends, and Lyrics* addresses this connection nicely in its discussion of the lore of the walnut tree:

> The Walnut has become in Europe, and especially in Italy, an accursed tree. The ancients thought it dear to Proserpine and all the deities of the infernal regions. In Germany, the Black Walnut is regarded as a sinister tree, just as the Oak is looked upon as a tree of good omen. At Rome, there is a tradition that the church Santa Maria del Popolo was built by order of Paschal II., on the spot where formerly grew a Walnut tree, round which troops of demons danced during the night. Near Prescia, in Tuscany, we are told by Prof. Giuliani, there is a Walnut tree where witches are popularly supposed to sleep: the people of the district say that witches love Walnut trees. (Folkard, 1884)

Why are demons, which are so frequently the old spirits of the pagan world transformed into new roles, said to dance about the central point of a tree? Why do the spirits of witches here take their rest?

Figure 15. Witches feasting under a tree. Adapted from *De Lamiis et Pythonicis Mulieribus* (1489).

We should not imagine that the walnut tree is the only type associated with witches and devilry, for any modern witch familiar with the old lore can name others, including the infamous examples of blackthorn, hawthorn, and willow. The laws of King Cnut, who ruled in Britain from 1016-1035, outlawed spiritual worship of all trees more broadly:

> We earnestly forbid every heathenism:
> heathenism is, that men worship idols; that
> is, that they worship heathen gods, and the
> sun or the moon, fire or rivers, water-wells
> or stones, or forest trees of any kind; or love
> witchcraft, or promote morth-work in any
> wise.

The phrase "morth-work" in the above passage should be read as "murder-work," illustrating the connection between the old animist practices, witchcraft, and the use of curses and poisons that would have been known during Cnut's age. Folkloric fragments give us a piece of the truth, but our work here is to unify them so that we might better understand our Devil as a whole, and to that end, we must unpack the connection between the tree's symbolism and the Devil of lore and legend.

We cannot ignore one of the most enduring biblical symbols connected with him: the tree of knowledge. On the surface level, this myth preserved in Genesis is a familiar one. The Devil, in the form of a serpent, tempts Eve with fruit from the tree of knowledge, and despite knowing that she is forbidden to eat of it, she succumbs to this temptation and shares the fruit with Adam, resulting in their expulsion from paradise and the origin of death and toil in the world. The identification of the serpent with the Devil, though, is not biblical, but *folkloric*. Nowhere in the text is this being identified as the Devil, and yet, this reading has been accepted for ages. Perhaps it is because the serpent, being able to tunnel beneath the earth, was in previous ages associated with the forbidden knowledge of the otherworld, or perhaps it is because, in shedding its skin, the serpent was associated with rebirth. (What is their expulsion from the garden if not a kind of rebirth?) Rabbinical perspectives regard the serpent in Eden as the embodiment of human desires and temptations rather than as an external being of evil.

In any case, this tree that conveys knowledge, and with it the autonomy to choose good or evil for oneself, plays a role in the development of early humans in this tale. Upon eating its fruit, Adam and Eve become self-aware, realizing their own nakedness, which is in a poetic sense the realization that one *can be clothed*, an important developmental benchmark for humanity, resulting in less exposure to the elements. What's more, they realize that they will die. This awareness of our eventual death is crucial to the nature of humanity as we know it; without it, we are little more than animals. Similarly, they are told that they will now toil, signaling a shift from hunting and gathering towards the labor of agriculture.

Figure 16. Arbor Scientiae. Adapted from *Ars Magna* (1295).

Read in this way, the tree and the serpent do not spell human ruination, but rather, human development. We are no longer ignorant, no longer entirely like other animal creatures; we cannot simply dwell in the garden as other creatures do, gathering food when we are hungry, entrusting ourselves and our well-being to the whims of nature. Our intelligence compels us to plan and to toil, for we know and understand the reality of death, and we are aware of ourselves as human. Our knowledge of good and evil allows us to act with agency rather than instinct, with deliberateness rather than animal grace. We are now subject to death because we now *understand* death, for the tree has somehow changed us into a new kind of creature, one more cunning and capable—in short, a creature of craft.

The role of trees in the anthropological and spiritual development of humanity has been long attested by scholars and folklorists alike. Frazer (1890) notes the significance of trees to ancient man, inviting us to imagine an older world in which far larger areas of western Europe would have been dense with forest. It is only natural then, he suggests, that these towering giants that covered most of the landscape would be perceived as powerful spirits. They could provide shelter, food in the form of nuts and fruit, medicine, and the wood necessary for cooking and safely consuming meat. Their fell branches could be crafted into all manner of tools. Their rootedness in unseen kingdoms below and the far reach of their branches into the sky would have signified their otherworldly properties. In short, trees could easily have been the first gods of humanity. This early animist approach to understanding tree spirits involved a careful spiritual respect for these beings:

> To the savage the world in general is animate, and trees and plants are no exception to the rule. He thinks that they have souls like his own, and he treats them accordingly. "They say," writes the ancient vegetarian Porphyry, "that primitive men led an unhappy life, for their superstition did not stop at animals but extended even to plants. For why should the slaughter of an ox or a sheep be a greater wrong than the felling of a fir or an oak, seeing that a soul is implanted in these trees also?" (Frazer, 1890)

Frazer notes the concept of trees having a shared governing spirit, not bound within the physical being of the tree itself; this is a later form of animism that would have served as a foundation of polytheism. This development is much more like the modern forms of animism practiced by witches today.

Returning to our question of why the devils dance about the tree and why the witches rest there in Folkard's account, we see that the tree serves as a spiritual nexus for older spirits observed by mankind, and that the tree itself carries the old spiritual memory of its previous roles as provider, protector, and deity. These concepts did not die in the development of our diverse cultures, but colored and influenced the folklore surviving today regarding trees and their spirits.

We see vestiges of our old tree gods in the living folk traditions of the May pole and May bush. Walsh (1897) describes the way previous generations might have observed the connection between the May pole and the pagan rituals of past ages:

> The Maypole was usually made of birch, and adorned with flowers and ribbons. In the villages it was often set up for the occasion of May-Day Eve, but in London and elsewhere there were Maypoles permanently standing in the streets. It was only natural

that the May revels should invite the condemnation of the Puritans. Stubbes in his "Anatomy of Abuses" (1583) amiably characterized the Maypole as a "stinckyng idol" which the people bring from the woods, "following it with greate devotion." And when they have set it up they "leape and dance aboute it, as the heathen people did at the dedication of their idolles."

Although not noted by Walsh, modern witches are well aware of the continuation of this tradition today alongside the practice of adorning the May bush, which is usually a small tree or shrub decorated with ribbons or scraps of fabric. This ritual simultaneously recognizes the animating spirit within the tree or plant and identifies it with a larger spiritual principle active throughout nature, the pole, tree, or shrub becoming emblematic, signifying an Old One so ubiquitous and ancient as to be without a modern name, and yet somehow deeply connected to the memory of the primordial tree as an ancient being itself, a personality awakening with the coming of summer, an entity important, somehow, to those phantom traces of who our animist ancestors were.

Nor are these symbols confined to the rites of witches; we see the spirit of the tree honored even in the commercialized practice of the modern Christmas tree, and we smile in a knowing way as witches when we witness the inevitability of these continuing symbols even among those who do not see their underlying meaning.

The symbol of the evergreen, which endures the season of death unchanged, expresses itself in many currents of lore, but perhaps none so pointed as in *Sir Gawain and the Green Knight*, an Arthurian legend from the late 1300s with an unknown author. The Green Knight is an enigmatic character in the story, but reveals himself as a threshold guardian, testing Sir Gawain's worthiness and honesty. He is unable to die, living even after public decapitation at a Yule feast, echoing the vital flourishing of evergreens in winter. We can view his challenge to Gawain in broader terms as the test the human spirit must face against the unpredictable forces of the wilderness, and in this way, the knight's code that must be upheld in order to survive his challenge is civilization itself pitted against the lawless wilds. In addition, the Green Knight is, of course, a being connected to witchcraft itself, being enchanted by Morgan le Fay. Even in this transformed state, we see the figure of the spirit in the green serving as both challenger and teacher, enemy and ally, personified in a being who is reborn in the same way nature is reborn. Tales like this one would have spoken to medieval folk with familiar themes, echoing folk-religious traditions and spiritual practices grounded in the natural world.

Nor is the dark time of the year, the dangerous season of winter, with its biting cold and fallow crops, without its own more frightening iterations of our Devil. It is not without meaning that we find the Krampus, the yule-tide Devil eager to punish and terrify, associated with the season most inclined to cause hardship for ancient peoples. Similarly, we find the Mari Lywd or Grey Mare of Welsh tradition, a grim figure made from horse's skull carried on a pole, decorated often with fabric or ribbons. In the United States, a spirit of this same vein exists by the name of Belsnickel: a ragged, terrifying figure who chases children with a whip (Ridenour & Tejaratchi, 2016). These spirits are all distinct, but share in their ghoulish imagery the ache and fear that the season of winter would have represented to ancient generations less comfortable than we.

This personification of the green world appears also in the imagery of the Green Man, usually a face made of leaves, carved into various churches and buildings across the ancient and medieval world. It is worth noting that ancient carvings of this well-known motif appear more human. As medieval Christianity increasingly identified old pagan practices as devilry, iterations of the Green Man carved into churches in the medieval period become more grotesque and demonic, the character of our Devil similarly solidifying around these peripheral elements of folk-magical practice and animist folk-belief, encompassing an expanding menagerie of heretical concepts: the sacred wilds, the spirits of the natural world, the folk magics of what came to be called "witchcraft" in this period, and even our pagan ancestors themselves.

Although we must exercise skepticism when reading the ancient Roman accounts of the Druids (since they were biasedly characterized as a barbaric enemy of the empire), the infamous account of the wicker man from 1 B.C.E. has had a lasting impact on cultural memory. In his description, Caesar describes how the druidic priests erected a humanoid figure made of wood, filled it with human offerings, and lit the figure on fire.

Given the wealth of surviving folk customs related to burning effigies, including corn dollies, it is more likely that this figure was not filled with humans at all. We can also speculate that this effigy was, if anything, representative of the green world's culmination and cyclical decline into winter.

Figure 17. The Wicker Man or Wicker Image.
Adapted from *A Tour in Wales* (1778).

Ritualistic violence in association with cults of the green world would have been perhaps more familiar to the Greco-Roman world than to the Celtic world. The maenads, the legendary followers of Dionysus, were said to tear men to shreds, devouring their flesh and blood in a state of spiritual ecstasy brought on by their wilderness god. Dionysus' worshippers were said to carry a sacred staff called a thyrsus, decorated in leaves and vines. Many of the symbols of Dionysus were, of course, syncretized with the Roman Bacchus, who remained a god of wine, vine, and vegetation, and also a dying god who is reborn in the same manner as the green world. Even his epithets, "endendors" (of the tree), "phleus" (of the bloom), and "thyllophorus" (having leaves) echo his role as a green world entity. Scot (1584) in his *Disoverie of Witchcraft* even recognizes documented observations of the connection between these ancient cults and the lore of the witches' sabbat:

> Psellus addeth hereunto, that certeine magicall heretikes, to wit; the Eutychians, assemblie themselves everie good fridaie at

night; and putting out the candles, doo commit incestuous adulterie...cutting their children in peeces, fill their pots with their bloud; then burne they the carcases, and mingle ashes therewith, and so preserve the same for magicall purposes. Cardanus writeth (though in mine opinion not verie/probablie) that these excourses, dansings, etc.: had their beginning from certeine heretikes called Dulcini, who devised those feasts of Bacchus which are named Orgia, whereunto these kind of people openlie assembled; and beginning with riot, ended with this follie. Which feasts being prohibited, they nevertheless hanted them secretlie; and when they could not doo so, then did they in cogitation onelie, and even to this daie (saith he) there remaineth a certeine image or resemblance thereof among our melancholike women.

The phrase "cogitation" here is important, for it suggests an event held in a state of dream or dream-like trance. Scot is observing here the popular belief that witches participated in a dream sabbat built of vestiges of cultural memory, an ancient remembrance of pagan gatherings held in the past. In physical ritual, however, we see even stronger connection to modern folk-religious practice among witches and non-witches alike; the wine-god cult's ritual use of alcohol, representative of the vine's spirit being imbibed by the dedicant, suggests early forms of what would later, through a merging of various pagan cult themes, become the ritual of the eucharist, which was revised and diversified in a variety of folk practices.

In fact, this act of imbibing the juice or body of the plant as sacred communion is far from unique to Christianity, for it is a basic animist principle observed in diverse cultures that as we imbibe the fruits of the land, we participate in its cycles and partake of its spirit. This idea is preserved in folk traditions of wassailing, which originates in a ritual of singing to the trees of the orchard to "wake" them and ensure good apple production for the year ahead. In modern practice, folk and traditional witches often pour a measure of wassail or steeped cider at the roots of old apple trees in order to honor the spirits of the land on which they reside.

The ancient spirits of the vegetable world recognized in folk rites are not necessarily male, though, as evidenced in traditions of the corn mother. Writing of northern European customs, Frazer (1890) writes:

> Further, the Corn-mother plays an important part in harvest customs. She is believed to be present in the handful of corn which is left standing last on the field; and with the cutting of this last handful she is caught, or driven away, or killed. In the first of these cases, the last sheaf is carried joyfully home and honored as a divine being. It is placed in the barn, and at the threshing the corn-spirit appears again...In the neighborhood of Danzig the person who cuts the last years of corn makes them into a doll, which is called the Corn-mother or the Old Woman and is brought home on the last wagon. In some parts of Holstein the last sheaf is dressed in a woman's clothes and called the Corn-mother. It is carried on the last wagon, and then thoroughly drenched with water. The drenching with water is doubtless a rain-charm.

It is in the form of braided wheat and similar charms that these traditions of the corn-mother can be said to exist in other European traditions. Whereas the May pole or bush represents the body of the green world in its expansion into summer, the corn dolly represents the soul of the land's harvests taken indoors to preserve its seeds for the coming year.

The old song of John Barleycorn preserves the spirit and meaning behind many of these practices (though perhaps in a more playful way), identifying the body and the soul within the grain and acknowledging the land cycles responsible for the production of ale. Here I include the 1782 version by Robert Burns in full, since its imagery and sounds are so enjoyable and valuable to modern witches:

> There was three kings into the east,
> Three kings both great and high,
> And they hae sworn a solemn oath
> John Barleycorn should die.
>
> They took a plough and plough'd him down,
> Put clods upon his head,
> And they hae sworn a solemn oath
> John Barleycorn was dead.

But the cheerful Spring came kindly on,
And show'rs began to fall;
John Barleycorn got up again,
And sore surpris'd them all.

The sultry suns of Summer came,
And he grew thick and strong,
His head weel arm'd wi' pointed spears,
That no one should him wrong.

The sober Autumn enter'd mild,
When he grew wan and pale;
His bending joints and drooping head
Show'd he began to fail.

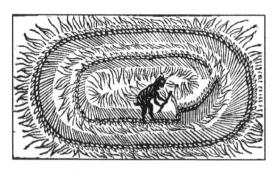

Figure 18. Old Nick harvesting grain from a farmer's field. Adapted from *The Mowing Devil: Or, Strange News Out of Hartfordshire* (1678).

His colour sicken'd more and more,
He faded into age;
And then his enemies began
To show their deadly rage.

They've taen a weapon, long and sharp,
And cut him by the knee;
Then ty'd him fast upon a cart,
Like a rogue for forgerie.

They laid him down upon his back,
And cudgell'd him full sore;
They hung him up before the storm,
And turn'd him o'er and o'er.

They filled up a darksome pit
With water to the brim;
They heaved in John Barleycorn,
There let him sink or swim.

They laid him out upon the floor,
To work him farther woe;
And still, as signs of life appear'd,
They toss'd him to and fro.

They wasted, o'er a scorching flame,
The marrow of his bones;

But a miller us'd him worst of all,
For he crush'd him between two stones.

And they hae taen his very heart's blood,
And drank it round and round;
And still the more and more they drank,
Their joy did more abound.

John Barleycorn was a hero bold,
Of noble enterprise;
For if you do but taste his blood,
'Twill make your courage rise.

'Twill make a man forget his woe;
'Twill heighten all his joy;
'Twill make the widow's heart to sing,
Tho' the tear were in her eye.

Then let us toast John Barleycorn,
Each man a glass in hand;
And may his great posterity
Ne'er fail in old Scotland!

In the eyes of church officials in those ages
past, harvest-charming traditions would have been
viewed as continuations of some ancient devilry,

charms and witchcraft of the same variety outlawed by Cnut. The identity of the witches' Devil, swollen to encompass these themes and practices related to the green world, becomes even more complex now, a figural archive containing vestiges of nature spirits, charms of harvest and natural cycles, and the human symbiosis with the land. In preserving the place of the Devil in our craft, we preserve, in part, these traditions of charming.

This relationship of symbiosis between human practitioners of witchcraft and the spirits of the green world and the harvest is an important one in modern practice, and its implications provide context for understanding certain passages of witch-lore held sacred to us. Among these, the conjuration of the meal given in *Aradia* holds a special enshrined place in witchcraft spirituality:

> I conjure thee, O Meal!
> Who art indeed our body, since without thee
> We could not live, thou who (at first as seed)
> Before becoming flower went in the earth,
> Where all deep secrets hide, and then when ground
> Didst dance like dust in the wind, and yet meanwhile
> Didst bear with thee in flitting, secrets strange!

> And yet erewhile, when thou wert in the ear,
> Even as a (golden) glittering grain, even then
> The fireflies came to cast on thee their light
> And aid thy growth, because without their help
> Thou couldst not grow nor beautiful become;
> Therefore thou dost belong unto the race
> Of witches or of fairies... (Leland, 1899)

There are several elements in this passage that are important to our understanding of the Devil's handprint in the green world. In the first stanza, we see again, much like in John Barleycorn, the personification of the grain as a being, an entity distinct unto itself, again echoing animist themes that are present throughout folk craft as a whole.

We also see a key connection drawn between this charm and the eucharist, that instead of partaking in the body of Christ, witches are recognizing the dependence of their body upon the land and the nourishment it provides. This charm is, like much of lore-based craft, partly heretical. To subvert liturgical symbolism in this way is to reposition Christianity as merely another magical language, not a sacred cosmology or truth, but merely something of use to the practitioner in a given moment. Christianity is often seen in folk craft as simply another set of symbols available for use in the charming arts. Ironically, it is in subverting the symbol of the eucharist that this charm reveals an actual truth at the core of it, echoing the many pagan rites of sacred eating and imbibing that informed the development of this sacrament later in the Christian religion.

Another key layer at work in this charm is the recognition of chthonic powers in relationship with the abundance of the land. The grain goes into the earth, "where all deep secrets hide," much like the serpent and hare who tunnel below ground, and also, of course, like the dead themselves.

Most importantly for our purposes, we see the relationship that "light" has with the spirit of the grain in this charm. The fireflies that cast their light upon the grain are recognized, like witches and faeries, as beings of light in *Aradia,* light or "splendor" being elsewhere identified in the manuscript's lore as the distinct quality of Lucifer, embodied as light itself (Diana being the darkness within which it shines). Like witches and faeries, the fireflies are beings that hold within them the contrast of light and darkness, ruled over by both a fallen angel and a dread queen.

At last, this pursuit of the Devil's symbol and lore as a green spirit brings us to one of the most well-known, though usually incomplete, fragments of fable related to his nature: the jack-o-lantern. This name is related to the tale of Stingy Jack described previously in our exploration of the Devil as a bound spirit, but it has had other names over the ages: Will-o-wisp, Will-o-torch, Jack and his Lantern, and most notably, "Hob and his Lantern" (Allies, 1852). This name, which echoes the nickname of the Devil as the "Old Hob," reveals something deeper at work in the folk tradition of the vegetable-as-lantern.

Figure 19. Modern jack-o-lantern beside its older cousin, the "hob and his lantern." Older forms of the jack-o-lantern were often carved from root vegetables.

In lighting our candle within the gourd or turnip, we do more than create a light in the darkness; we recognize with the symbol of light the spirit within the fruit of the land itself, that it is a living presence that must rot and die, only to return. We erect, whether we are aware of it or not, a fetish to the green spirit identified as "Old Hob," and we keep an animistic vigil for the Old One within the land.

Perhaps, in light of the ways the green world has over time become such a part of our Devil, we modern witches can resist the urge to sanitize the plant kingdom in our magics. "Green" is often used in modern craft to describe branches of practice that are considered more wholesome and less dangerous, more "light" and less "darkness," usually with little mention of our Devil at all, but perhaps we should not hold such assumptions about the green craft. We see in these patterns of lore how some of the oldest definitions of witchcraft in the English language included the Devil in the spirits of the green world, how the entities of nature merged and synergized with this concept, how the chthonic underworld, in its relation with the dead, is also by folkloric connection bound up with the Devil's domain under the earth. Folk craft is, at its core, a syncretic spirituality, a faith stitched like a patchwork quilt from both the heretical parts of

Christianity and the old animism of the pagan world, and if we remove the Devil from the green, we ignore this rich and unique complexity in our heritage.

Figure 20. Two witches attend to their cauldron-work. Originally
adapted from *De Lamiis et Pythonicis Mulieribus* (1489).

Divine Poison

The vast legacy of the witch's art of poisoning is preserved in language itself. The infamous biblical phrase, "thou shalt not suffer a witch to live" translates the Hebrew *mekhashepha* as *witch*, though its connotative meanings point more directly to *poisoner*. The folkloric thread connecting poisons, witches, and the Devil is neither coincidental nor simple, for as we shall see, it relies on older concepts of the venomous aspect of the divine and preserves aspects of his nature that would have been better understood by people living hundreds of years in the past.

Even in the early modern period, popular minds connected the poisoning arts directly with the arts of witchcraft:

> Sometimes a murtherer with poison is called a witch. Sometimes they are so termed by verie signification of their names; as Elimas, which signifieth a sorcerer. Sometimes they studie curious and vaine arts. Sometimes it is taken for woonding or greeving of the hart. Yea the verie word Magus, which is Latine for a magician, is translated as witch; and yet it was heretofore always taken in the good part. And at this daie it is indifferent to saie in the English toong; She is a witch; or, She is a wise woman. (Scot, 1584)

It is not without reason that Scot's contemporaries in the 1500s associated poison with witches.

The mythic witch Medea utilizes her arts to poison the dress gifted to Glauce, an act of vengeance after Jason leaves her for his new bride. Circe utilizes poisons to transform the men who invade her island into beasts. (As an interesting side-note, it has been speculated that the original plant in this myth may have been henbane, a psychoactive nightshade historically identified as "hog-bean."

Figure 21. Black henbane. Adapted from *Nouveau Dictionnaire Encyclopedique Universel Illustre* (1891).

Poisoning with nightshade alkaloids has been noted to induce irrational, destructive, beast-like behavior.)

Early modern witchcraft trials involving an amalgam of both poisoning and sorcery are common, as in the 1607 trial of Bartie Paterson:

> In a case of mixed poisoning and witchcraft which occurred in 1607, no moral distinction appears to have been made between the

administration of potions destined to kill and potions destined to cure. The adoption of means held to involve unlawful and supernatural agency, was held to be the moral offence, not affected by the ultimate temporal result. Thus Bartie Paterson, tasker in Newbottle, is accused "of the crime of sorcery and witchcraft, in abusing of the people with charms and divers sorts of inchantments, and ministering, under the form of medicine, of poisonable drinks... (Burton, 1852)

Even Cotton Mather (1862), in *The Wonders of the Invisible World,* associates witchcraft with a kind of poisonous devilry:

Men consult the Aspects of Planets, whose Northern and Southern motions receive denominations from a Celestial Dragon, till the Infernal Dragon at length insinuate into them, with a Poison of Witchcraft that can't be cured.

In the minds of peoples living in western Europe from the 1300s to the 1800s, there was little difference between poisoning by herbal preparation and poisoning by a malefic charm. For common folk, the chemicals by which monkshood, foxglove, and deadly nightshade caused death did not need to be understood; it was enough to know that contact with these plants could cause harm. In the same way, having a witch's charm placed on one's property or her powders or oils scattered on one's person was known to enact the curse.

This principle of causation, often called *contagion*, is still instructive for practicing witches today. Like *sympathy* or *simulacra*, it is a sort of magical law governing principles of craft. The principle of contagion posits that, on a basic level, magical properties can be transferred via proximity or touch. In the cursing arts, it is not merely that spiritual poison has been hurled at the target (though it can certainly be this), but often that *the witch herself becomes, on some level, poisonous to the intended victim.* This is the hidden logic behind so many simple maledictions in witch-lore that require only one's speaking voice. In these acts of magic, the witch's very words and breath become toxic to the victim, an embodied baneful magic that allows the practitioner to become, for a moment, poison made flesh. Nor did the magic of the curse isolate itself once imparted, but instead often affected a spread and a contagion to everything loved by the afflicted, as in the following malediction:

> Curssed be they in the field, in the grove, in the woods, in their houses, barnes, chambers, and beds; and curssed be they in the court, in the waie, in the towne, in the castell, in the water, in the church, in the churchyard, in the tribunall place, in battell, in their abode, in the market place, in their talke, in silence, in eating, in watching, in sleeping, in drinking. in feeling, in sitting, in kneeling, in standing[,] in lieng, in idlenes, in all their worke, in their bodie and soule, in their five wits, and in everie place. Curssed be the fruit of their wombs, and curssed be the fruit of their lands, and curssed be all that they have. Curssed be their heads, their mouthes, their nostrels, their noses, their lips, their jawes, their teeth, their eies and eielids, their braines, the roofe of their mouthes, their toongs, their throtes, their breasts, their harts, their bellies, their livers, all their bowels, and their stomach.

Curssed be their navels, their spleenes, their
bladder. Curssed be their thighs, their legs,
their feete, their toes, their necks, their
shoulders. Curssed be their backs, curssed be
their armes, curssed be their elbowes, curssed
be their hands, and their fingers, curssed be
both the nails of their hands and feete;
curssed be their ribbes and their genitals, and
their knees, curssed be their flesh, curssed be
their bones, curssed be their bloud, curssed
be the skin of their bodies, curssed be the
marrowe in their bones, curssed be they from
the crowne of the head, to the sole of the
foote: and whatsoever is betwixt the same, be
it accurssed, that is to saie, their five senses;
to wit, their seeing, their hearing, their
smelling, their tasting, and their feeling...
(Scot, 1584)

Charms would certainly be vocalized in earshot of
the victim, but may also be spoken to a
simulacrum or image stand-in baptized in the
victim's name. The significance and diversity of
the poisoning arts as an aspect of old witchery has
been immortalized in the folkloric text of *Aradia*
by Charles Godfrey Leland (1899):

And thou shalt be the first of witches known;
And thou shalt be the first of all i' the world;
And thou shalt teach the art of poisoning,
Of poisoning those who are great lords of all;
Yea, thou shalt make them die in their palaces;
And thou shalt bind the oppressor's soul (with power);
And when ye find a peasant who is rich,
Then ye shall teach the witch, your pupil, how
To ruin all his crops with tempests dire,
With lightning and with thunder (terrible),
And with the hail and wind...

And when a priest shall do you injury
By his benedictions, ye shall do to him
Double the harm, and do it in the name
Of me, Diana, Queen of witches all...

Appropriately, the poisonous plants with which we interact in our craft are often named after our Devil, signifying both their danger and their sorcerous capabilities, but also perhaps suggesting something else. By observing the ways plants named after our devil grow and thrive, how they pollinate, fruit, and defend themselves from danger, we can actually glean something of the nature of our Devil himself. The infamous datura stramonium, for example, also known as devil's snare or devil's trumpet, protects its seeds with vicious thorns. Disturbing the plant releases a strong odor that has been compared to the smell of feet (though in my experience, it is more of a nutty, musky scent).

Figure 22. A mandrake. Adapted from *Hortus Sanitatis* (1497).

The plant's chemical constitution is so strong that breathing the scent from a damaged root can send blood rushing to the cheeks and effect a mild disoriented feeling (which is not entirely unpleasant, but is not at all recommended due to the inherent dangers of this poisonous plant). At night, its pale, ghost-like blossoms gently open, mimicking the grace of the moon above and welcoming its favorite pollinators: moths.

The magic of this plant lies somewhere between its alluring flowers and its deadly weaponry, and the ecstasy this plant brings (when prepared safely by one with experience) is derived fully from its poisonous nature. In preparing ointments, tinctures, and essences, the wise witch follows carefully a trusted recipe, observing proper dilution so as to avoid harm without neutering its power. Arousal, this plant seems to say, has something to do with danger itself. Ecstasy is tempered by the slightest touch of anxiety. Desire itself, which we human beings imagine so often to be the opposite of fear, is actually amplified by danger when it is controlled and reduced to circumvent actual harm. It is impossible not to liken this to witchcraft and to the arts of our Devil. It is impossible not to see the connection to our own magics as we call to dark spirits, to the dead, to realms of power described as full of horrors, knowing that the ecstasy and power we seek lie somewhere beyond them, that only by reaching into the dark and wild can we ever succeed in claiming the prize. The lesson here, which is the importance of temperance or dilution, speaks to our position as belonging both to the other and to the human, to ourselves and to our shadowy kin. Many of these plants offer similar, though distinct lessons, each of them holy:

Devil's Apple (Mandrake)

Devil's Bit (a name referring to a great many plants, including Scabious, Dita Tree, and Bluebonnet)

Devil's Bite (Snakeroot)

Devil's Claw (Club Moss)

Devil's Curse (antiquated name for Ergot poisoning)

Devil's Dung (Asafetida)

Devil's Ear (Wake Robin)

Devil's Eye (Henbane)

Devil's Garters (Convolvulus)

Devil's Guts (Dodder)

Devil's Herb (Deadly Nightshade)

Devil's Ivy (Pothos)

Devil's Mushroom (various Psilocybin fungi)

Devil's Plaything (Yarrow)

Devil's Ribbon (Toadflax)

Devil's Tobacco (various species of Wild Tobacco)

Devil's Trumpet (Thornapple)
Devil's Walkingstick (Angelica Tree)

The astute reader will quickly note how many of these plants are either outright poisonous or psychoactive (and usually poisonous in the wrong preparation or dosage). In observing these plants with the eyes of a witch, we note their strange patterns of growth. While plants producing safely edible berries entice us to consume their fruit in order to pass their seeds through our digestive systems and proliferate the species, deadly nightshade (Devil's herb) tempts us in order to overcome us. Its seeds, carried inside the tempting berries, grow not only from the passing of waste, but from the corpse of the victim who falls prey to this enticement. Its natural design seeks to make of us (or those foolish enough to eat the fruit) a cradle for its young.

We are not, by this lesson, the center of creation. We are not the pinnacle of any food chain or of any imagined hierarchy of beings. We are vulnerable, and a simple plant can subdue us as easily as a lion or wolf.

Figure 23. Atropa belladonna or deadly nightshade. Adapted
from *Neu Vollkommen Kräuter-Buch* (1731).

In resisting this knowledge through willful
ignorance, we die; in accepting it, we are able to
procure carefully some of the most valuable
remedies and magical herbal preparations from our
would-be poisoners.

    Likewise, many plants named after the Devil
are aggressive in their growth patterns,
overthrowing crops and proliferating themselves at
an alarming pace. These plants, while problematic
for farmers, offer us a necessary truth: that for all
of our efforts at order and control, we are never,

in the end, the masters of this earth. We are limited in terms of what we can control, for nature has its own designs and its own patterns, and we are ultimately at the whim of larger forces. In resisting this knowledge, we create poisons for our crops that do more harm than good. In accepting it, we learn to focus our efforts, to turn our attention towards small-scale, localized farming and gardening, to what we *can* control with reasonable effort, allowing ourselves to live alongside the wilderness rather than fighting an exhausting, harmful, and truly futile battle against it.

Despite the fact that many of these plants are dangerous, they have been used in medicinal preparations for hundreds of years, and they have allayed endless suffering and saved countless lives in their skillful use by those with the knowledge to do so. Grieves (1931) notes that henbane, through its hyoscyamine and hyoscine alkaloids, has been used against muscular spasms, pain due to cystitis, and even in cases of anxiety and irritable cough. Mandrake has been used historically for convulsions, rheumatism, depression, and chronic pain (Grieves, 1931).

Today, mandrake, thornapple, henbane, deadly nightshade, and other plants of our Devil are wisely utilized in the form of external applications (unguents and balms), homeopathic remedies, flower essences, and tinctures that have been carefully diluted so as to achieve their effects without risk of poisoning. In the hands of those with the necessary knowledge, these poisons become potent allies. Our larger question, really, is why beneficium and maleficium, benevolent power and malevolent power, are so often bound up together in the same vessel, for in this truth, we see the fingerprint of our Devil yet again.

One answer to this question lies in the tension between stasis (stillness) and kinesis (movement) when observed as spiritual principles echoed in the biological world. In a state of stasis, we are untouched and uninfluenced, much like Adam and Eve in the story of Eden, sealed away with no means to experience pain. But this security comes with a cost, for without anything at stake, we are also unable to experience true exhilaration and true ecstasy, for these things require an element of risk, an element of danger that involves us letting go of ourselves for a moment in order to step outside of ourselves. Kinesis, on the other hand, brings transformation, both immediate and long-term, and its effects are quickening and often pleasurable, but its price is danger, the possibility of not only being aroused, healed, or strengthened somehow, but being utterly annihilated. Both forms of transformation—for good and ill—are forms of change. And so, when we say that a plant belongs to the Devil, what we really mean to say is not that the plant is altogether wicked or ruinous in every circumstance, not that it is always harmful, but that it is always *potent*. It is *potent* for change, for transformation, for affecting human existence on a profound level. Its impact will be strong, and it will be felt. Its properties interrupt stasis and yield something different, something other, a new state of being. Whether it is poison or cure depends on our skills and our approach, but either way, the Devil's plants are *potent*.

The spiritual property of potency has been observed historically by a variety of cults in the ancient pagan world, most notably around substances that result in inebriation. We must differentiate briefly here between *psychoactive* and *psychedelic*, though, since all of these substances would be considered psychoactive, but few would be truly psychedelic. *Psychoactive* merely means affecting or altering consciousness, not necessarily inducing hallucinations or profound inebriating effects. Coffee, tea, and tobacco, for example, would be considered psychoactive (and have, in fact, been revered as sacred plant spirits in ancient cultures), but we would not consider them psychedelic. Regardless of this fact, coffee, tea, and tobacco are all poisonous in sufficient amounts, exhibiting harmful effects on the body when imbibed in great quantities. Our goal here is not to outline various ways of "getting high," but to try to understand how ancient cults that formed around psychoactive plant spirits came to influence the character of our Devil over time, becoming ingrained in his lore.

Of those ancient cults, Dionysus and his maenads (or Bacchus to the Romans) bear perhaps the most direct mythic relationship with our Devil. We have already discussed how the witches' sabbat was imagined in early modern times to be born of an "ancient memory" of inebriating and sensual pagan ceremonies. The specific points of overlap, though, are compelling. His orgiastic, nocturnal rites held at Parnassus bear more than a fleeting resemblance to descriptions of the witches' sabbat in early modern times (Smith, 1871). The predominance of women among his worshippers offers another important point of overlap, as well as his cult's emphasis on freedom and the release of the constraints of society. His status as the god of the vine and the importance of wine as his "body" in his ecstatic celebrations would have presented an anachronism in the eyes of the early modern church that required explanation. For them, the similarity between the Dionysian rites and the eucharistic ones of the church would have been nothing but diabolical, evidence of the Devil mocking the foreknown arrival of Christ. As ridiculous as this conclusion may seem today, this perspective cemented Dionysus and Bacchus, the wild gods of ecstasy in the ancient world, as aspects of our Devil, bringing their myth and lore into the miasma of personalities that merged into his folkloric being. And yet, on a deep level, the Dionysian link to the eucharist makes a great deal of sense; in drinking the spirit of the vine in great quantities, inhibitions are released, and perception is altered. As an amalgam deity, Dionysus himself was the result of many layers of syncretism, absorbing local deities and morphing over time even before his introduction in ancient Greece. It is probable that his association with the vine is one of his most ancient and enduring aspects, and that the most primitive forms of his worship may have been as the spirit of the vine and the grape itself.

Similarly, the rites of Demeter and Persephone were said to revolve around inebriating substances. Their worship in the Eleusinian Mysteries was tied to that of Dionysus (Iacchus), but moreover, modern scholarship has unveiled the probability that worshippers of these two goddesses likely partook in the consumption of ergot, a psychoactive red fungus that is known to grow on grains (Wasson et al.). That Demeter was known as the goddess of the earth and its crops, and that Persephone was often metaphorically understood as rising with the crops after winter's slumber further cements the relationship between these two divinities and the psychoactive ergot. An initiate who imbibed ergot would doubtless experience profound (and perhaps terrifying) phenomena. Its ritual use would have lent an ecstatic component to the initiation rites at Eleusis. We know from the writings of philosophers that these rites were aimed at the perception of the immortal soul within the husk of the body, and though dangerous, the practice of deliberate ergot poisoning would have aided the initiate in the perception of the otherworldly truths they sought to witness firsthand. Both Demeter and Persephone have also been depicted in ancient art alongside poppy pods and flowers (Carod-Artal, 2013), suggesting another strong correlation to the well-known psychoactive papaver somniferum.

Though most of us understand Apollo as an ancient Greek god of music, art, medicine, and prophecy, he bore strong connections in ancient times with poisons and psychoactives. Scholars have posited that the oracle at Delphi, a priestess of the temple of Apollo in ancient Greece, utilized a form of datura preparation in order to receive her visionary messages from the god (Schultes, 1970). In metaphorical terms, though, it was understood that the priestess breathed the fumes rising from the slain body of Apollo's enemy, an ancient serpent, which rested at the bottom of a chasm beneath the temple. Plutarch described the "vapors" rising from fissures beneath as inducing the oracle's trance. One wonders whether the "fumes of the serpent" served as a symbol for the smoke of datura or for some other inebriating substance available to the priestess. Regardless, as a god of both prophecy and healing, Apollo's worshippers were likely to have been equipped with medicines that served multiple purposes, like the beautiful and dangerous datura—inebriating, medicinal, or poisonous, depending on preparation and dosage. It is notable here that Lucifer and Apollo share many qualities as ancient pagan personifications of light and illumination.

Less is known about the specific ritual practices of the Celts and the pagans operating in the Western European areas from which many of our ancestors came, but the few discoveries we have made are provocative. We know, for example, that nightshades likely served an important role in those pagan cults. Vessels have been discovered containing henbane seeds dating from the early Bronze Age (Ratsch, 2005). The plant was called *belinuntia* or *beleno* in Celtic regions, associating it with Bel, a solar deity. Henbane was burned as a fumigation as part of his worship, and the druidic practice of inhaling its smoke was known to transport the worshipper to a spiritual other world. Hemp fields in Switzerland are noted in local folklore as being a site of ancient pagan festivals, often referred to as a location for the "witches' dances." In fact, it is the association with witches that suggests ancient pagan usage for many plants, including datura stramonium. Ratsch (2005) posits that widespread belladonna use was unlikely, though, due to its particular dangers.

What matters most in our picture of the Devil as Divine Poisoner is the unity behind this portrait. From the fruit of the tree in Eden (which may represent a psychoactive plant) to the ritual use of entheogens in proximity to pagan deities that would later be syncretized in our Devil, we see the important role of these plants to his personality and his nature, understood as both dangerous and transformative, for good or ill, an interrupter of stasis and a shifter of consciousness. It is in this broader spiritual truth that we find the figure known as Samael, an angel whose name is translated variously as *Venom of God, Severity of God,* or *Poison of God.* In light of his roles and associations over time, I would like to suggest a fourth reading here and posit that we can perhaps best understand this spirit as the *Potency of God*.

In order to approach the concept of this being within Judaism and theology, we must turn to the 13th century *Yalkut Hadash*, which asserts that the angel Samael is "identical with the serpent" that appears in the story of Eden, going even further to posit that "Samael took his band with him and chose for himself the cunning and malicious serpent, mounted him and rode upon him down to earth." We can interpret this language as suggestive of spiritual transference, as "riding" is a metaphorical way of expressing the use of a physical being as a vehicle for a spiritual entity moving through and into the world. As the tempter of Eve, Samael has been suggested in Jewish lore to be the true father of Cain. In addition, Judaism has traditionally interpreted Samael as the angel of death, responsible for carrying out God's will in annihilating humans judged fit to die. Samael has been folklorically understood as the identity of the angel who tormented Job (with God's permission) and wrestled Jacob. Over time, perhaps over many generations of tellings and retellings, we see Samael assume the role of the leader of the fallen angels, becoming synonymous with Satan.

And yet, in the various roles of Samael, we find a kind of theological and cosmological fracture when viewed through the lens of Christianity. How can Samael be both a loyal servant doling out God's punishment and the enemy of God at the same time? Older concepts of deity were not so black and white, it seems; indeed, they left room for the possibility that death, suffering, and poison itself, though terrible, were also divine.

It is in the lore of the Qliphoth, originating in the 13th century *Zohar*, that we see Samael partnered with Lilith as a prime demonic ruler. In this union of the Poison of God and the First Woman (who can also be understood as the First Witch), we learn something more of Samael's true nature. We should read Lilith's union with Samael as a direct result of her assumption of power for herself. As she famously spoke a secret word or name of God in order to refuse Adam as her lord and master, she aligned herself not with the power of unity, but with division, not with subservience to greater divinity, but with the seeking of divinity within oneself. Though her alliance has shifted, her holiness is intact; she is aligned with the dark aspect of divinity, but is no less divine, merely transformed, operating within a different current of power than the one prescribed to her by others. Samael offers the path by which the first witch is both dark and divine at once, not divorced from spiritual power itself, but unified with it more fully according to her nature, which compels her to rebel, to refuse, and to assert her own independence from Adam and from the subservience of the garden.

As an aspect of our Devil, we see how even Samael and the theological texts analyzing his nature complicate the picture of the "enemy of God." The Devil we see here is adversarial, but not evil; dark, but not without divinity; dangerous, but not without purpose. His influence offers, evenhandedly, two possibilities: that we may ruin ourselves, or that we may ascend to power. Perhaps to Samael, the outcome is irrelevant. Perhaps his nature is the potency for change, for transformation, and perhaps the way in which we are transformed, becoming either darkly divine or a moldering corpse, is in our own hands. Perhaps, like the poisonous plants touched by our Devil, he merely *is*, and it is in how we respond to his influence that we become either empowered or annihilated.

There are many parallels in this lesson. Since we understand that poison and medicine in fact arrived together and not separately in humanity's development (healing and baneful preparations often coming from the same plant), we can view veneficium as a cornerstone of civilization. Other important societal developments pose no less danger, and offer no less in the way of reward. Fire destroys and ravages as easily as it cooks, warms, and lights our way in darkness. Agriculture itself is capable, as it often does today, of ravaging and ruining the earth when wielded irresponsibly. The arts of metalwork can and do render terrible weapons as well as beneficial tools. Viewed from the wider lens of other societal developments, the arts of poisoning are, once again, an example of the entrustment of humanity with something that could spell boon or bane, a gift that affects agency. We are permitted, like Eve in the garden, to choose for ourselves rather than live in blind faith and subservience. We are empowered and entrusted, and though we may destroy ourselves if we act without wisdom, we may also preserve ourselves. Like so many gifts of our Devil, the power is placed in our own hands, and we are offered the freedom to live or to die. The heart of the gift, it seems, is neither malice nor comfort, but merely potency. We alone must decide, then: potency for what?

Figure 24. The Devil conducts his heretical sermon in place of a priest.
Adapted from *The History of Witches and Wizards* (1720).

Primus Magus

We should not ignore the fact that the Devil was imagined, in early modern times, to be a sort of heretical spiritual leader, mimicking the practices of the church in a subverted and sinister way. The description of Barbara Napier in North Berwick, 1590, echoes many of the beliefs of the time:

> ...the devil wess with them in likeness of ane black man...the devil start up in the pulpit, like a mickle blak man, with ane black beard sticking out like ane goat's beard, clad in ane black tatie gown and ane ewill favoured sscull bonnet on his heid, hauing ane black book in his hande...

While we can safely assume that some elements of Napier's imagery here are being prompted by her tormentors, this is entirely beside the point. She is being steered (to what degree we cannot say) towards popularly accepted views of the Devil as a spiritual entity at this time in Scotland.

These folk beliefs surrounding the Devil are confirmed in Isobel Gowdie's testimony as well, famously given of her own free will:

> ...We get al this power from the Divell, and when ve seik it from him, ve call him "owr Lord." At each tyme, quhan ve wold meitt with him, we behoowit to ryse and mak our curtesie; and we wold say, "Ye ar welcome, owr Lord" and "How doe ye, my Lord."

It is no wonder then, given the belief that the Devil operated on his own spiritual current antithetical to the church, that Gowdie recounts so many charms utilizing the phrase "in the Divell's name." One finds iterations of charming in his name all over the world, in fact; in Guernsey in 1563, witches were said to use the phrase "va au nom du Diable."

Much like the church-derived and folk-magically appropriated "in nominee Patris et Filii et Spiritus Sancti," this empowerment of the Devil's very name with a potency for charming is a call to a greater body, an alignment of the self in magical acts with an entity more ancient and potent to which one in some spirit belongs, not quite so different from listing the names of one's parents or ancestors to establish a kind of inherited authority, an aristocratic (or in this case chthonic) line ending with the witch.

The Devil appears in older lore as a figure of magical leadership and tutelage, but his role is markedly unlike that of a god. He is not all-powerful, but executes his will on the world through specific magical arts. He is not distant, but immediate and personal in his interactions with his witches. He is not a creator, but a mentor and a founder. He is not a judge or establisher of morality, but a teacher who offers lessons in arts that may be used for good or ill. He was believed, for example, to have taught the Somerset witches of the 1600s to baptize wax images in the names of victims (Murray, 1931). The Devil interacts with the world, if we are to believe the old lore, through his very witches, such as the Basque witches who were even noted to say, as they anointed themselves, "I am the Devil. I have nothing which is not thine." In exchange for specific offerings and regular spiritual engagement, which is the true form of nourishment for the oldest spirits of this world, the Devil was believed to offer witches a belonging, a communion, a place in an ancient, timeless lineage of sorcerous practitioners. Evidence for this relationship of exchange is plentiful in the old lore, including a witch at Burton-on-Trent in 1597, who was said to ask for a "penny to bestow" in return for her healing services.

Despite the fact that the Devil overwhelmingly does not perform the role of deity, he is nonetheless a figure of reverence whose rites become mingled and blended with those of the church in more than one strand of lore. It is in this blending that we find the liturgical or "popish" charming arts that have had such an enduring presence in folk and traditional craft. What does the aspect of the Devil as First Heretic mean for witches today who practice magical psalmistry, who call upon the saints, who make the sign of the cross and utilize rosaries or the many forms of folk-charming beads syncretized with the folk rosary tradition?

These matters are complicated, and in order to understand them, we must go further still. The *Compendium Maleficarum* of Guazzo (1608) admits and attempts to explain how witches syncretize craft with elements of faith:

> Most cunningly does Satan, that Master of perversity, mask his magic under the appearance of religion: and this he does, both that he may the more easily lead into superstitious error those who are naturally disposed to that cult; and that, by himself working miraculous cures, he may avert suspicion from his followers...For witches observe various silences, measurings, vigils, mutterings, figures and fires, as if they were some expiatory religious rite...Most intolerable of all, they often mingle with their prayers all sorts of filth...

We can very clearly discern from passages like this one that witchcraft "experts" at the time were very much concerned about folk magic. In addition to their delusional hunt for a unified, malevolent witch-cult, they were possessed of a very real fear about religious language and symbols being appropriated into remnants of pagan magic, being mixed with the occult, and being utilized by the lower classes to achieve magical power. The spiritual syncretism of Christianity with old pagan animist remnants, a natural event when the tides of religious power shift in a culture, was viewed as the work of the Devil himself.

To this day, there is some element of secrecy in rural, religious places when it comes to the private use of liturgy and psalmistry as a magical act. It is viewed as either superstitious or somewhat heretical to speak religious words with occult power in hand and worldly gains in mind. The liturgical charming arts ingrained in folk magic are not at all of the same flavor as evangelical Christian prayer. They are spoken secretly rather than loudly, over candles instead of on stages. There are charms for healing, but also for cursing and tormenting one's enemies. And for the folk witch, there often lies in the words a lingering flavor of heretical intention, as if the entity petitioned under the title of "Lord" is not quite the same as the one named in a church, as if the prayer were being worked in a secret way somehow, given a new meaning in our mouths, addressing a different sort of power.

In American folk magic, the use of the psalms has a long history, informed certainly by British immigrants, who brought their cunning craft overseas, but also by German folk magic and, over time, infused with African and Native American spiritual practices in the traditions of hoodoo and some forms of brujeria, these two currents often recognized as sister traditions to the cunning branches of folk witchery. Magical psalmistry today stands as one of the commonalities uniting diverse folk traditions that are otherwise quite distinct.

One source commonly recognized in Appalachian folk craft is the infamous *Sixth and Seventh Books of Moses*, an 1849 text from Germany which included in an older edition a version of the *Sepher Shummush Tehillim*, a treatise on the magical use of the psalms originally published in the 1500s.

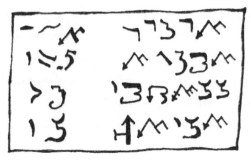

Figure 25. Seal for the general citation unto spirits in the *Sixth and Seventh Books of Moses* (1800s).

The text illustrates the ways the psalms were (and still are) utilized magically for a variety of purposes, for both good and ill:

> Psalm 4: For excellent luck and success in all endeavors.
>
> Psalm 7: Against enemies who seek to do harm; to render their efforts impotent.
>
> Psalm 22: Against misfortune and harm while traveling.
>
> Psalm 23: For instruction via visions or dreams.
>
> Psalm 31: Against slander and harmful speech.
>
> Psalm 47: To be beloved and respected by others.
>
> Psalms 53 to 55: A series of psalms to subvert the efforts of enemies. The first

silences enemies and fills them with fear. The second brings vengeance against them. The third is a terrible curse.

Psalm 60: For victory in battle and against injury.

Psalm 65: For good fortune in all undertakings.

Psalm 70: To conquer one's enemies.

Psalm 74: Against oppression by rich and heartless persons. Also to bring them a terrible end.

Psalm 78: To be beloved by those in power.

Psalm 79: A fatal curse against enemies.

Psalm 85: For reconciliation with former friends.

Psalm 89: Against grave illness. Also for liberation from imprisonment.

Psalms 96 and 97: For family joy and contentment.

Psalms 102 and 103: For fertility.

Psalm 110: To compel all enemies to submission.

Psalm 112: For power and influence.

Psalm 114: For success in one's trade or business.

Psalm 118: To silence the enemy.

Psalm 120: For favor in legal matters.

Psalm 126: For the health of one's child.

Psalm 128: For a safe and healthy pregnancy.

Psalm 130: To pass by enemies unseen.

Psalm 134: For success in academics.

Psalm 139: For love between couples.

Psalm 141: Against fearfulness and anxiety.

Psalm 147: Against venomous bites and deadly wounds.

The *Tehillim* includes magical purposes for every psalm, but the text itself should not be considered perfect and absolute. This grimoire lists, for example, the thirtieth psalm as an effective incantation against evil, but it is also for certain a potent charm in necromancy, for it contains the compelling lines "thou hast brought up my soul from the grave." The psalms need not be recited wholly or as printed in any version of the bible, but can, in the heretical charming arts, be excerpted, abbreviated by utilizing the first letter of a series of passages, or reversed. This latter option is merely another iteration of the infamous witch's prayer (the Lord's prayer pronounced backwards) applied here to psalmistry instead. The contemplation of the strange sounds produced by reversing a psalm create a meditative sequence for

the witch and a potent (if at times challenging)
incantation to pronounce over one's workings.

Tipeh et oht nawad ohg
tohn doush ee taat eveelah
ahm tapek tasah ooth ehvarg
et morf loos eyem pah torb
tasah ooth dro lo

Figure 26. Psalmic reversal charm derived from Psalm 30:3,
a call to the spirit from the grave.

For the folk witch interested in magical psalmistry,
it is preferable and recommended to *actually read*
this ancient book of incantations for oneself in
order to identify the potent passages and their
suggested applications.

Traditional witches often describe the
relationship between popish charms and diabolism
in our arts as a "crooked path," interpreted in
modern language as a serpent winding its way to
and fro, between Heaven and Hell, God and the
Devil. Though it is an easy way to explain a

complex subject to outsiders, I sometimes find this very binary model to be somewhat inaccurate. Syncretic spirituality is usually not a back-and-forth oscillation, full of sharp pivots between ideologies, but rather, a comfort in lasting folk tradition, an acknowledgement that this heretical charming, this subversion of faith, is simply part of who we are and where we come from. The practitioner is not torn between two directions, but confident in one. It is this gray area in which our cunning folk ancestors dwelled, and it is where our power often lies, somewhere between and behind the paradigm of Heaven and Hell, salvation and damnation. In short, heretical charming (and this could be said of many other elements of syncretic spirituality) is not quite this and not quite that, but is instead something *other*.

Our Devil is closely associated with this blended manner of charm-work, due in no small part to his role as First Heretic, the first mythic figure to commit disobedience to the Judeo-Christian God despite his position as angel. Returning to our chapter on the Bound Spirit, we see Azazel named as the leader of the rebellious angels in the *Book of Enoch*, but this name is listed as one among a host of other spirits found guilty of disobeying God by teaching and empowering mankind with forbidden knowledge:

> And Azazel taught men to make swords, and knives, and shields, and breastplates, and made known to them the metals (of the earth) and the art of working them, and bracelets, and ornaments, and the use of antimony, and the beautifying of the eyelids, and all kinds of costly stones, and all colouring tinctures. And there arose much godlessness, and they committed fornication, and they were led astray, and became corrupt in all their ways. Semjaza taught enchantments, and root-cuttings, Armaros the resolving of enchantments, Baraqijal taught astrology, Kokabel the constellations, Ezeqeel the knowledge of the clouds, Araqiel the signs of the earth, Shamsiel the signs of the sun, and Sariel the course of the moon...

The association of Azazel with metal-work is interesting here. In ancient Greece, Hades was associated with the working of precious metals, hidden as they are in the dark world under the earth's surface, nearer to the land of the dead. To manipulate metals requires a forge, of course, which is perhaps why many witches read Azazel here as a spirit bearing the fire of cunning.

We see the name Azazel echoed in another interesting context in Leviticus as a sacrificial figure. In ancient Judaism, this spirit was associated with Yom Kippur, and it is in fact the root of the concept of a "scapegoat"—a goat burdened with all the sins of the community, which is chased away into the wilds and cast over a cliff to die so that the people may be cleansed of their iniquities. The similarly named Azrael is present in Islam as an angel of death, described as having one foot poised on a bridge thin as a razor's edge dividing Heaven and Hell.

Modern traditional witches who appreciate this mythic thread have interpreted a sort of lore-born ancestry of witchcraft between the lines of these ancient texts, suggesting a "line of Cain." This is not and should in no way be interpreted as a literal ancestral claim, but rather should be appreciated as a poetic statement of origin, an alternative interpretation of ancient myth in order to illustrate the connection between the modern witch and the many ancient figures tied to our

Devil through folkloric readings. In this view, Cain is actually begotten either by the serpent in the garden or by the fallen angels who are described in the Book of Enoch as mating with humans. The murder of Abel is an inversion of cosmological order; the offering of blood unto the land instead of unto God, which was customary at the time. Though cruel, this act is nonetheless magically potent for Cain, for it confers the blessing given to Abel by God for his sacrifice back to the land itself, establishing Cain as conduit for that power, a death-and-renewal myth echoed in folkloric songs and tales like John Barleycorn. Rather than an actual human victim, Abel becomes, in this reading, a symbol for life given by and returned to the soil. For this crime, Cain's line is "marked," and writers in the 14-1800s noted the similarity here to the fabled witches' mark. Cain's punishment is to live forever, but to wander endlessly in a desolate landscape, a description evocative of (and later, folklorically connected with) the moon. He becomes, in the course of time, merged with the Norse Mani and emerges folklorically as the Man in the Moon. At the same time, Cain is seen as the first human member of his own diabolical ancestral line, including later the legendary metal-worker Tubal Cain and many of the kings and queens of the old pagan world, who are viewed as ancestors in the witches' line.

These mythic and folkloric readings of the Devil as First Heretic and original imparter of the cunning fire reveal yet another of his roles: Primus Magus, or First Sorcerer. This role, too, likely arose from a moment of syncretism in the collision of Christianity and the old pagan animism. Thompson (1919) notes the prevalence of horned figures painted in caves and on stone cliffs across western Europe, most likely representing early shaman-like practitioners from prehistoric times. To communities transformed by the spread of Christianity across Europe, these figures would have looked something like the Devil indeed, and so what may have simply been a minor figure appearing occasionally in biblical text became something more: a potent, sorcerous being, whose emblems are ubiquitous in ancient ruins and desolate places, an older spirit somehow connected to magic itself and to our own ancestors. That this figure would be recognized in folklore as the spiritual leader of witches and warlocks is no surprise.

What may surprise some, however, is the folkloric understanding of his role as Founder of the Hosts of Faery. We have already established the connection between witches and faeries as two lines attributed to the Devil, but a Scottish oral account in *The Fairy-Faith in Celtic Countries* (1911) divulges more clearly the folkloric connection between Lucifer and the hidden people:

> The Proud Angel fomented a rebellion among the angels of heaven, where he had been a leading light. He declared that he would go and found a kingdom for himself. When going out at the door of heaven the Proud Angel brought prickly lightning and biting lightning out of the doorstep with his heels. Many angels followed him—so many that at last the Son called out, "Father! Father! The city is being emptied!" whereupon the Father ordered that the gates of heaven and the gates of hell should be closed. This was instantly done. And those who were in were in, and those who were out were out; while the hosts who had left heaven and had not reached hell flew into the holes

of the earth, like the stormy petrels. These
are the Fairy Folk—ever since doomed to live
under the ground, and only allowed to
emerge where and when the King permits.

Even our ancestors, it seems, understood that the
lines between categories of spirits can be blurry,
that faeries and demons are names given to
describe a variety of spiritual entities that bear
similar hallmarks. And in the syncretism of the
old animism and the new faith, they sorted out
their own answers, reasoning poetically rather than
religiously the chasm between these two worlds.

Figure 27. Witches gathered with spirits. Adapted from
The Devil in Britain and America (1896).

This connection between the Devil and the
fae is echoed again in the ballad of Tam Lin in a

brief but important reference to a tithe (or in Burns' version, a "tiend") to Hell:

> And ance it fell upon a day,
> A cauld day and a snell,
> When we were frae the hunting come,
> That frae my horse I fell;
>
> The Queen o Fairies she caught me,
> In yon green hill to dwell.
> And pleasant is the fairy land,
> But, an eerie tale to tell,
>
> Ay at the end of seven years
> We pay a tiend to hell;
> I am sae fair and fu' o flesh
> I'm feared it be mysel.
>
> But the night is Halloween, lady,
> The morn is Hallowday;
> Then win me, win me, an ye will
> For weel I wat ye may. (Burns, 1897)

This ballad, itself a tale of otherworldly encounter with the spirit-as-lover, captures a popular folkloric motif. The infamous "tithe to Hell" was said to be paid by the fae every seven years in the form

of a captured human soul. This payment allowed
Elphame or fairy land to continue its existence as
a subterranean realm somewhere near the threshold
of Hell, but not within it, imagined as a sort of
colony, or perhaps imagining the denizens of faery
themselves as tenants to the Devil.

For folk witches like myself, who draw our
charms profusely from the early modern period
and from the lands our cunning ancestors walked
during this age, the role of the Devil as Founder
of Faery is significant. For one thing, it draws an
interesting parallel with the tale from *Aradia* in
which Diana assumes her role as queen of both
witches and faeries. In this understanding, faeries
become more than a footnote in witch-lore,
something akin to a sister race, a sibling nation
of magical beings much like ourselves, existing
somehow outside and between both Heaven and
Hell under the tutelage and guidance of both the
Devil and a dark queen.

And here we have it: the Devil as a leader of
wild and unruly magical spirits, as chief of spirits
yet again, in a new role, and as master of the
magical secrets they keep; as first sorcerer and
heretic, who first assumed his own power separate

from God's, an example followed by his devils, by his faeries, and by his witches as well, the human iteration of an otherworldly magical race, the body of a heretical church somehow perpetually betwixt and between.

This stream of folklore affirms yet again the animist view of faeries as spirits of the dead, a matter about which I've written before, but a point that bears repeating. Lang (1888) offers the following helpful passage in his discussion of the 17th century fairy tales of Charles Perrault:

> In the mediaeval form of Orpheus and Eurydice (Orfeo and Heurodis), it is not the King of the Dead, but the king of Fairy that carries off the minstrel's bride. Fairyland, when Orpheus visits it, is like Homer's Hades...In the same way Chaucer calls Pluto 'King of Fayrie,' and speaks of 'Proserpine and all her fayrie,' in the *Merchant's Tale*. Moreover Alison Pearson, when she visited Elfland, found there many of the dead, among them Maitland of Lethington, and one of the Buccleughs. For all this dealing with fairies and the dead was Alison burned.

Passages like this one, along with the many accounts of witches interacting with the dead, offers one clue. Another is bound up in the "faerie hill" said to be their residence in the lore, which is, in fact, a burial mound. It is near the old mounds and crumbling structures of previous ages that these spirits are most often said to dwell, pointing to spiritual interactions with the forgotten ancestral dead. We even recognize in older pagan deities that became synthesized with our Devil a role as leader of the dead or "chief of the mound"—

> The god most prominently set forth in early Irish missionary records, in the Lives of the Saints, and in the ancient Bards, is *Crom, Cromm Cruach*, or *Cenn Cruach*, the bleeding head; or *Cromm Cruaich*, the Crooked or Bent One of the Mound...He is associated with Mag Slecht, a mound near Ballymagauran, of Tullyhead Barony, County Cavan. The Welsh god *Pen Crug* or *Cruc*, Chief of the Mound, answered to the Irish deity. (Hyde, 1899)

This is the same Crom who was sometimes identified as Crom Dubh, or "Black Crooked One," a figure sometimes associated with older, pagan origins of Lughnasadh or Lammas.

Interestingly, the "elf darts" so often discussed in early modern lore and charms are actually prehistoric arrowheads used by ancient ancestors. They would have been (and still are) discovered near these prehistoric burial mounds, and thus, are quite literally the weapons of the dead. This understanding of the fae as spirits of the dead can be confusing in light of the previously highlighted lore identifying the fae as fallen angels, but we must remember that folklore is not paradigmatic, but pluralistic, revealing spiritual truths rather than empirical ones. Faeries are the ancestral dead; faeries are demons; faeries are land spirits. In folk craft, these statements do not contradict each other, but offer us a variety of lenses through which to understand these beings.

If we are to view the Devil properly as originator, founder, and first of the witches' line, we must turn to the examples in folkloric accounts of initiation for ways the witch is brought into the body of this ageless coven. We must differentiate these initiatory experiences from oath-bound initiations conducted in modern groups, for they are of a different nature entirely, as we shall see.

While much of the witch-hunting literature contains wildly diabolical (and unbelievable) descriptions of imagined initiation ceremonies, one of the more common threads is the renunciation of baptismal vows committed privately or in the presence of the Devil himself. This renunciation appears in Thomas & Thomas' (1920) collection of Appalachian superstitions as well as in Davis' *The Silver Bullet*, an influential collection of Appalachian witch-lore. We can trace this motif of renunciation very clearly to Scottish witch-lore, an example of which is found in the works of Sir George Mackenzie (1699):

> The Formula...[for the initiation of a new witch] is, I deny God Creator of Heaven and Earth, and I adhere to thee, and believe in thee...Renunciation of Baptism is by Delrio made an effect of Paction, yet with us it is relevant, per se...and the Solemnity confest by our witches is putting one hand to the crown of the Head, and another to

> the sole of the Foot, renouncing their
> Baptism in that posture...

The overwhelming majority of the accounts of
initiation in folklore involve only the witch in
question or the witch in communion with the
Devil or other spirits present. The position of one
hand placed over the head and another under the
foot itself suggests the lack of other attendants in
bodily presence; this is a rite of passage with no
other participants, at least on a physical level.

Conversely, the witch's initiation as a peopled
event is overwhelmingly modern. While it is
known that our cunning craft and folk-charming
ancestors perceived spirits and had knowledge and
power conferred upon them through those
relationships, there is no evidence of group
practices and memberships. True to its animist
roots, folk craft tends to emphasize initiation as
an ongoing series of revelations held in private, an
experience shared between the witch and the spirit
or spirits conferring wisdom and power along the
path. In folk craft, the term "self-initiation," used
frequently in Wiccan traditions, is an oxymoron,
for initiation is granted solely by our otherworldly
kin. These rites are unpeopled, but they are by no

means conducted alone; one cannot confer belonging upon oneself.

This contrast between belonging and otherness is consistent across witch-lore in various cultures. On the one hand, the witch belongs deeply to that invisible body of initiates lead by the Devil as Primus Magus, as founder and First Heretic; on the other hand, the figure of the witch recorded in lore and historical charming practices almost always conducts their work alone, at least in terms of human company, and is folklorically viewed as an outsider or other figure, often living a rural life on the edge of human society.

In Appalachian folklore, witches are made in a vast variety of ways that are themselves suggestive of simple rituals. The thrice renunciation of one's baptism is a frequent feature of these, as is the presence of water, suggestive of a "washing away" of previous baptismal vows to the Christian God. Other, less common forms of becoming a witch include the turning of a spinning wheel in the middle of running water, the use of a silver bullet to shoot a hole in a white handkerchief, and calling to the Devil on a mountaintop at sunrise (Davis, 1975). These practices draw in no small part on the folklore of Scotland and other cultures survived in the poor immigrants who were many of our ancestors, who purchased and worked the rocky, difficult mountain terrain there for lack of the money required to settle in easier places. The thrice renunciation alone echoes many elements of early modern Scottish witch-lore. These people, who often longed for home and kept the old stories and songs for love of their fading cultural memories, preserved such worthy jewels in their witch-lore, our inheritance.

In all of these oscillations, in all of these facets of our Devil as Primus Magus, we as witches are suggested to enter a kind of invisible covenant, an unseen company. While many forms of modern witchcraft focus on the building of a literal human company identified as a "coven," we see that the underlying *covenant*, which is the root of the former term and the key to its actual meaning, cannot be truly captured in a mere physical assembly of humans. The greater covenant of witches is ancient, a lineage mythically tied to our Devil, and its implications are far more vast and enduring. Its nature is spiritual rather than organizational; suggestive of magical access to a hidden culture, one recessed in deep and unconscious cultural memory, a door unlocked in the dark dream of our sabbat.

When we embrace the truth of ourselves as living participants in this mythic lineage, our craft is transformed. We are no longer like Prometheus stealing the fire from the gods, but are instead born of the fire ourselves, wielding the cunning that is, in a spiritual sense, our birthright. We are not liars or betrayers of baptismal vows (a common and unfortunate mistranslation of the origins of the term *warlock*), but are repositioned as loyal to ourselves, to where we come from, acting in continuity with the stories of those sorcerers and conjurers who came before us. We not torn between the liturgical and pagan-animist charming arts, but are firmly rooted somewhere between. In short, we are not alone, but arrive into ourselves through many voices, tales, and histories, dark and divine at once. The fears and anxiety that would limit our power find their release in this, for though the mysterious night is full of things that may harm us, the night itself is our parent, our mother and our father.

Figure 28. The Devil sits at the head of the feast at the witches' sabbat.
Adapted from *The History of Witches and Wizards* (1720).

Beast of the Sabbat

I n the antiquated testimonies of witch-lore, the Devil appears not only as a humanoid or goat figure, but in various animal forms. His bestial nature is not merely evidence of church officials reducing this figure to a sub-human status, but is in fact closely tied to his folkloric origins and offers a key to grasping his nature. We find in the testimonies of 17th century Scottish witch Isobel Gowdie that the Devil appeared to her variously: "somtym he vold be lyk a stirk, a bull, a deir, a rae, or a dowg" (Wilby, 2010). Isabel Becquet, in 1617, also echoes the theme of the Devil in the form of a bestial composite being:

> ...no sooner had she arrived there [at the
> Devil's Sabbat held at Rocquaine Castle]
> than the Devil came to her in the form of a
> dog, with two great horns sticking up: and
> with one of his paws (which seemed to her
> like hands) took her by the hand: and calling
> her by name told her that she was welcome:
> then immediately the Devil made her kneel
> down: while he himself stood up on his hind
> legs; he then made her express detestation of
> the Eternal in these words: *I renounce God
> the Father, God the Son, and God the Holy
> Ghost*; and then caused her to worship and
> invoke himself. (Murray, 1921)

We can with certainty set aside Murray's false
claim that the Devil at these rites was a human
being dressed in animal disguise, just as we can
set aside her errant hypothesis that witch trial
testimonies can be taken for literal fact; instead,
we can look to passages like the one above to
understand the folklore behind the symbols of our
Devil, to try to grasp how our Devil was
understood and perhaps even perceived in a
spiritual sense by those who claimed to have
encountered him. This particular image of the
Devil as a dog with horns and human hands at

the ends of his paws is powerful, if frightening. It also captures quite succinctly the folkloric and artistic representation of the Devil as having a monstrous body, made of an amalgam of human and animal parts. These depictions are on the one hand seemingly grotesque, but are on the other hand quite striking in their insistence on the Devil as a being made up of many other beings, as an entity tied to the diversity of nature and the primal animal world in which human beings still participate, no matter how hard we try to imagine ourselves as superior to coexisting creatures.

This connection between the spirit we call our Devil and the human-animal interdependence was perhaps more obviously meaningful to our animistic ancestors. They would have depended on the movements of herds for survival, hunting and trapping food for the community. Animals would have provided not only meat, but bones for the crafting of tools and hides for much-needed defense against the elements. The hunt would have been a dire duty, not a sport, its success or failure spelling the fate of many. And in order to excel at the hunt, our ancestors would have been required to understand their prey intimately; its tracks, its movements, its desires, its habitats, and its life cycle would have been necessary knowledge in this task.

Even centuries later in human development, medieval peasants would bring their animals inside during the winter to ensure their survival, sleeping next to their livestock in their small, dirt-floor dwellings on long winter nights. Today, mass-scale meat production removes everyday people from the realities of animal life, but for previous generations, all but the wealthy would have known how to breed, birth, raise, feed, shelter, heal, and slaughter animals. This knowledge was precious to our ancestors, and though we should not be so naïve as to believe that animal cruelty was not common, we can safely say that it was not as impersonal and capitalistic as it is today. To be birthed, raised, and slaughtered by the same human hand is, if anything, intimate. Humans and animals lived more closely than today, and the fact that human survival depended on relationships with animals was known and understood plainly.

This ages-old relationship has been hypothesized as one of the most important influences in the development of horned deities, including Thompson's (1929) interpretation of the prehistoric cave-painting known as *The Sorcerer*. This ancient depiction of a shaman donning the horns and skin of a prey animal communicates to us, even today, the intimate relationship early humans would have had with these animals, and suggests perhaps the shapeshifting and ecstatic rituals they might have employed in order to call to the animal's spirit. The fact that our Devil is so frequently depicted with horns is no accident, but evidence of the demonization of older, animistic concepts of deity survived in the form of folklore and myth.

Nor are horned deity depictions isolated events, limited to prehistoric cave-paintings and carvings. In the ancient world, deities as widely known as Zeus, Dionysus, Isis, Hathor, and Loki were depicted as having horns. The Celtic Cernunnos, an infamous if misunderstood figure, is not a distinct deity at all, but a title that simply means "horned one," the name itself appearing in only one instance beside these ancient images. It is likely that the Celts knew and revered many "horned ones," distinct spirits whose actual names are now forgotten. We have said before that the focus of this work is not on anything so broad as a "horned god," but rather on the evolution of our Devil, and this distinction remains important for this reason: the only thing these ancient horned depictions have in common, the only thing uniting all of the diverse and widely scattered horned figures is, truth be told, their horns. They are not, as Murray supposed, depictions of the same deity, nor are they representative of a fragmented ancient cult venerating a once-singular horned figure. The root of their development is something more basic, more instinctual, and more human, a connection more easily identified by our animist ancestors.

The ubiquity of horned deities in the ancient world is also, if we are to believe Frazer (1890), tied to the evolution of the crown as a symbol of leadership. In his famous analysis of "The King of the Wood," Frazer discusses how the priest of Nemi, dedicated to Diana, goddess of the hunt, secured and eventually passed on his crown:

> In this sacred grove there grew a certain tree round which at any time of the day, and probably far into the night, a grim figure might be seen to prowl. In his hand he

carried a drawn sword, and he kept peering warily about him as if at every instant he expected to be set upon by an enemy. He was a priest and a murderer; and the man for whom he looked was sooner or later to murder him and hold the priesthood in his stead. Such was the rule of the sanctuary. A candidate for the priesthood could only succeed to office by slaying the priest, and having slain him, he retained office till he himself was slain by one stronger or craftier...The post which he held by his precarious tenure carried with it the title of king; but surely no crowned head ever lay uneasier, or was visited by more evil dreams than his. For year in, year out, summer and winter, in fair weather and foul, he had to keep his lonely watch, and whenever he snatched a troubled slumber it was at the peril of his life.

Here, we see plainly the curious thread that Frazer tugs at. The king, ever hunted, wears his crown like a pair of antlers, and becomes the prey. The crown becomes at once a symbol of leadership and spiritual authority, as it would have to the shamans of old who donned the skins of animals, but it is also a reminder of our vulnerability, of our participation in the predator-prey web of life. The king is, it seems, as vulnerable as the stag that Diana hunts by the light of the moon. He is not separate from the animal world, but knit within it, not superior to its laws, but dependent upon them.

As cruel and barbaric as this ancient ritual seems to us today, it speaks to a potential continuity in the development of the horned figure. What would the horned headdress have represented to early humans if not the success of the hunt and the nourishment of the people, won by craft and spiritual communion with the animal world? What would that figure represent to its people if not leadership, foresight, and power over the animal world? What more potent symbol could there be for a king than the antlers of the stag? What better crown could there be to place upon that brow?

The reason the horned headdress was passed on to our Devil becomes plain to see. We must view the demonization of the horns in the same way we view the demonization of the whole lot of ancient pagan imagery in the early day of the church:

> The concept of the Devil was also aided by the development of the concept of evil demons. Again, this was a movement of Greek thought in the direction of dualism. At first demons are, like the original gods, morally ambivalent. Then two groups of demons are distinguished, one good and the other evil. Finally, a shift in vocabulary occurs. In the Septuagint, *the good spirits are called angels and the evil spirits demons.* Plutarch also opposes the demons to the gods. Both identify the demons as wholly evil spiritual beings. These are now easily amalgamated with the Devil, either lending their traits to him, or being spirits subordinate to him, just as the Watcher angels in the Apocalyptic literature became subject to Satan or Mastema. (Russell, 1977)

What this development posits is a gradual diabolization of the original Greek *daimon*, simply meaning divine spirit, into the modern concept of *demons*, being a host of evil beings infesting the world, much as the early Christians would have looked upon the plethora of deity statues, depictions, and carvings all around them in pagan cities as "demons," once sacred beings, but now recast as purely evil spirits opposed to the one God of Christianity. The fact that our Devil has horns is not, it turns out, a uniquely identifying feature of this spirit, but rather, the result of the pagan ubiquity of horned figures. Our denigration of the sacred horned figure is evidence of society's widescale rejection of a once-sacred truth: we are animals ourselves, even the best of us, bound to them in survival and subject to the same natural laws to which they must answer.

This villainization of horned pagan imagery is ironic in no small part due to the fact that horns feature heavily in the bible, both as an offering to God and as a symbol of holiness itself:

> And they brought seven bullocks, and seven rams, and seven lambs, and seven he-goats, for a sin offering for the kingdom, and for the sanctuary, and for Judah. And he commanded the priests the sons of Aaron to offer them on the altar of the Lord. (2 Chronicles 29:21)

> And thou shalt take of the blood of the bullock, and put it upon the horns of the altar with thy

finger, and pour all the blood beside the bottom of the altar. (Exodus, 29:12)

His glory is like the firstling of his bullock, and his horns are like the horns of unicorns... (Deuteronomy 33:17)

But my horn shalt thou exalt like the horn of an unicorn: I shall be anointed with fresh oil. (Psalm 92:10)

Arise and thresh, O daughter of Zion: for I will make thine horn iron, and I will make thy hoofs brass... (Micah 4:13)

And his brightness was as the light; he had horns coming out of his hand: and there was the hiding of his power. (Habakkuk 3:4)

And I beheld, and lo, in the midst of the throne and of the four beasts, and in the midst of the elders, stood a Lamb as it had been slain, having seven horns and seven eyes, which are the seven Spirits of God sent forth into all the earth. (Revelation 5:6)

In addition to being associated with animal sacrifice in early Hebrew faith, which much more closely resembled other ancient pagan-animist ritual practices, the sacredness of horned spirit imagery retained its potency even in early Christianity. The Abrahamic faiths have, after all, like all other religions in the world, developed from what was once a more basic and less ornate form of animist spirituality. Although the ancient Hebrews decried neighboring religions for worshipping the bull-horned deity known as *Baal*, this name can also be rendered *Bael*, as it appears later in demonological texts, containing within it the name *El*, denoting *lord*. This is the same root found in Hebrew divine titles for God such as *El-Shaddai* and *Elohim*. Even in the late 1200s, scholarship has noted that "some Israelites, under the influence of their neighbors, identified their own god Yahweh with Baal, the principal god of the Canaanite pantheon" (Patai, 1973). Even within the Abrahamic faiths, there endures still today a suppressed cultural memory of the sacredness of the human-animal connection, the symbolism of the hunt, and the relationship between divine lords and the precious mantle of the horns.

For modern practitioners of the cunning arts, this is a potent truth indeed, for it complicates the entity to whom the psalms are directed and suggests that syncretic aspects of our faith are not adulterations of a once-pure form of Christianity, but rather, the recognition of enduring, ancient concepts of deity that survive in these ancient sacred texts. In a sense, the use of liturgical charming and heretical psalmistry is not a departure from the sacred literature of the Abrahamic traditions, but rather, a recognition of their complexity and the pluralism inherent in the concept of "God" itself and the ancient horned figures who once shared in that title.

But it is not simply in his horned nature that our Devil earns his title as Beast of the Sabbat; his nature, as previously noted, is indeed an amalgam of animal parts, a monstrous body that represents the bestial, wild, and uncontrollable aspects of nature outside of society's rules and walls. We can see clear parallels in depictions of the Devil and various monstrous chimeras from artists of the medieval and early modern periods: snarling mouths, claws, and scales drawn from a diverse array of beasts. That which is meant to frighten the viewer in the Devil's imagery is ultimately drawn from the horrors of the animal world, of dangerous venomous and carnivorous creatures that capture a primordial fear of predators. These elements remind us, even at an unconscious level, of human frailty and vulnerability, that we are not the pinnacle of the food chain, that we can still be, despite the hard-won advances of civilization, prey. The fact that the beastly amalgam is organized into a humanoid figure touches another point of anxiety deep within us, suggesting that we are still animals ourselves, inseparable from that wilderness and the brutality of nature itself.

Within the category of bestial shape-shifting spirits, one such entity that has survived in fable and has recently enjoyed an elevated status in folk witchcraft is the Puca (also rendered Bucca or Pookha, depending on the region). In Celtic faery lore, the Puca appears as a jet-black goat, horse, dog, bull, or humanoid figure. As a shapeshifter, he is described as taking different forms in different settings. His nature is neither entirely malevolent nor benevolent, but complex, offering either boon or bane depending on how this spirit is approached by humans. Yeats' (1888) translation of the tale of the Piper and the Puca offers an insightful glimpse into this being's nature as an aspect of our Devil:

> In the old times, there was a half fool living in Dunmore, in the county Galway, and although he was excessively fond of music, he was unable to learn more than one tune, and that was the "Black Rogue." He used to get a good deal of money from the gentlemen, for they used to get sport out of him. One night the piper was coming home from a house where there had been a dance, and he was half drunk. When he came to a little bridge that was up by his mother's house, he squeezed the pipes on, and began playing the "Black Rogue." The Puca came behind him, and flung him upon his own back. There were long horns on the Puca, and the piper got a good grip of them, and then he said—
>
> "Destruction on you, you nasty beast, let me home. I have a ten-penny piece in my pocket for my mother, and she wants snuff."
>
> "Never mind your mother," said the Puca, "but keep your hold. If you fall, you will break your neck and your pipes." Then the Puca said to him, "Play up for me the 'Shan Van Vocht' (an t-seann-bhean bhocht)."

"I don't know it," said the piper.

"Never mind whether you do or you don't," said the Puca. "Play up, and I'll make you know."

The piper put wind in his bag, and he played such music as made himself wonder.

"Upon my word, you're a fine music-master," says the piper then; "but tell me where you're bringing me."

"There's a great feast in the house of the Banshee, on the top of Croagh Patric to-night," says the Puca, "and I'm bringing you there to play music, and, take my word, you'll get the price for your trouble."

It is no wonder that folk witches conceive of the Puca as an aspect of our Devil. Here, he takes the form of a black goat or bull and becomes a sort of psychopompic figure carrying the protagonist away to the hidden gathering of spirits that was and remains analogous to our witches' sabbat.

In this tale, the Puca is also depicted as a master of skill and knowledge, able to confer upon the musician the talent necessary to play his music. In this, he is close to the Devil of American folklore, who so frequently appears as a crafty figure, a trickster who is not merely gifted in the ways of the arts, but is in fact their source, music and similar arts being so often described as sinful by the church in previous ages.

Other beast-like and variably "monstrous" spiritual beings persist in folklore, carrying within them their own truths related to our Devil. Among these, we find Herne the Hunter, a horned figure leading the procession sometimes called the Wild Hunt (and other times explained as originating in the ghost of a fallen hunter).

Figure 29. Witches fly to the sabbat on a variety of vehicles, accompanied by spirits. Adapted from *The History of Witches and Wizards* (1720).

American folklore has no shortage of localized devils and goat-men who embody a mingled anatomy of human and animal. Though these entities are often described as "cryptids," suggesting a literal, biological creature yet to be discovered by science, we can better understand them as spiritual entities embodying a lost interdependence between the human and animal world. The fact that our beast-men persist in the folklore of so many lands and cultures is no surprise to us, then. As witches, we see in these images the echoes of those first masters of cunning and craft, those ancestors who first donned the animal hides and antlers, who performed the first ancient magics, the lineage we name as our very Devil, so basic to who we are that they cannot be erased, surviving still in the unconscious well of dreams and phantoms, that place where, for those with the skills, they can still be conjured into our presence.

One of the more interesting examples of this very connection lies in the spirit known as Janicot, whose name appears in witch-lore from 1609 associated with sabbatic revels among Basque witches, most often in the form of "Ianicot" (Murray, 1921). The name *Janicot* itself has been hypothesized as both a corruption of *Jaincoa*, the

Basque word for God, and a derivation of *Janus/Dianus*, a two-faced deity that predates the Latin era itself. Among other variants of his name, we find "Petit Jean," "Beau Janicot," and eventually, "Basajaun," a name that persists to this day in Basque folklore to describe human-like creatures covered in hair, quite similar in appearance to Bigfoot, who were said to have once taught early humans the secrets of metalwork and farming (Lurker, 1987).

Figure 30. Janus head.

Unfortunately, most writers on the topic of Janicot seek to prove the existence of a hidden biological species or an ancient, unified cult of worship; both of these pursuits miss the point entirely. What we have in Janicot is a well-preserved ancient memory of the first sorcerers of old, who were beast charmers, and a traceable progression of this cultural memory as it evolved into pagan god, Devil, and cryptid. In short, the evolution of Janicot captures the way the early modern church saw the Devil as something intrinsic to early human spirituality, something our pagan ancestors recognized as potent and sacred rather than shameful, a spirit dwelling both within us and outside of us, accessible at a level that is instinctual and primal to who we are.

It should come as no surprise, given what we understand about the development of demonology, that we see Bifrons among the hordes of dark spirits described in the *Goetia*. Bifrons is noted as a teaching spirit with knowledge of the arts and sciences, as well as an understanding of the properties of plants and stones, but it is his name that is most interesting here, for it is derived from the Latin word for "two-faced" and is easily traceable to titles for Janus used in antiquity, the same Janus who lies at the root of our Janicot. The demon Bifrons is said in the grimoires to appear as either a monstrous beast or a man, and this dual nature speaks here again to that point of anxiety and discomfort that the church suffered four hundred years ago, the recognition of the human-as-animal, of the human beast itself, a sacred interdependence that is one of the most ancient lessons offered by our Devil.

This aspect of our Devil has lent itself to a variety of shapeshifting charms and lycanthropic lore, both tales of humans who transformed into beasts and actual occult charms for assuming animal consciousness in an ecstatic state for magical purposes. In 1589, Peter Stumpp, also known as the werewolf of Bedburg, was believed by authorities to have been given a charmed belt by the Devil which allowed him to transmogrify into a great beast—

> "...the likeness of a greedy, devouring wolf, strong and mighty, with eyes great and large, which in the night sparkled like fire, a mouth great and wide, with most sharp and cruel teeth, a huge body, and mighty paws..."
> (Sidky, 2010)

Stumpp was executed on charges of both lycanthropy and witchcraft, and his case reveals the ways these two concepts were perceived as interrelated in the sixteenth century. A witch could, by certain occult means, take on the likeness of an animal, and a werewolf was often either a practitioner or a victim of witchcraft.

In the infamous *Compendium Maleficarum*, Francesco Maria Guazzo (1608) addressed the common belief that witches could transform into various beasts, arguing that this form of witchcraft consisted of illusion or the donning of some form of magical disguise (which, quite ironically, is somehow both far from and very near to the truth):

> No one can doubt but that all the arts and metamorphoses by which witches change men into beasts are deceptive illusions and opposed to all nature...The belief in such monstrous transformations is nothing new, but was firmly held by the Ancients many ages ago. Euanthes, an author of great note, says that it is recorded in the Annals of Arcadia that there was a certain family of the tribe of Anthus which used every so many years to go to a certain pool across which, having taken off their clothes, they swam, and they were at once changed from men into beasts: and after nine years, if they had not in that time tasted human blood, they returned to their former shape. Herodotus in

> *Melpomene*, and Solinus in the *Polyhistor*,
> chapter 8, record that the Neuri, who live by
> the river Dnieper, are changed into wolves on
> certain days in the year, and after the
> appointed time has elapsed they return to
> their true shape.

While modern witches can confirm that it is, in fact, physically impossible to become another organism entirely, Guazzo of course misses the point in these tales. Lore points not to empirical truth, but to spiritual truth; The long history of shapeshifting as a magical practice is not rooted in the desire for physical transformation, but a yearning for the experience of animal consciousness, to feel within oneself the strength of a bear, the ferocity of a wolf, the cunning of a cat, or the freedom of a bird, and to learn thereby those secret truths known only to creatures that embody these qualities, to know them intimately, to commune with them in that hidden wisdom. As modern witches know, this is a perfectly practical aim with considerable rewards for those who make the effort.

The fact that our Devil appears in a myriad of bestial forms is no mere effort to terrify. It is evidence of sorcerous mastery, symbolic of those ancient shamans in early human development who donned the hides and the horns. This facet of his nature speaks to a primal piece of the witch's soul, inviting us to take part in a communion not only between the human and the divine, but including all the world of fauna, recognizing that deeper truth of our interdependence, of the debt we owe to each other living creature in this world, and of our responsibility to respect other sentient beings. Our dreaming sabbat, the deep and true sabbat of ecstatic, otherworldly bliss, is not merely a human experience, but an animal one as well.

Figure 31. A witch conjures a storm at sea. Adapted from
Historia de Gentibus Septentrionalibus (1562).

Serpent in the Deep

In one of the rare cases of voluntary witchcraft confessions, Marie Lamont, in 1662, described both her workings and an unusual epithet for the Devil who taught and guided her in her craft:

> [She went out] in misty mornings with a hair rope (harrie tedder), which she was to draw over the mouth of a mug, saying, "In God's name, God send us milk, God sent it, and mickle of it." By which she means she and Kattrein got much of their neighbor's milk which they made into butter and cheese. Also she said, that two years and a half since, the devil came to them at Kattrein Scot's house, where many of them were present, and gave them all wine to drink and wheat bread to

> eat, and they danced and were very merry,
> the devil shaking hands with them, and she
> delivering herself over to him in baptism.
> And at her baptism she was given the name
> of "Clowts," and bid to call the devil
> "Serpent." (Linton, 1861)

The use of the rope in order to steal milk (in other words, to steal the abundance of another family) is no surprise here. This manner of charmwork also survives in Appalachian witchery and in many other veins of craft, brought over by Scottish immigrants, through the "milking" of tassels or rags in order to draw the victim's abundance or life force for oneself. What is unique here, at least on the surface, is the naming of the Devil as "Serpent," though we shall see that our Devil's connection to serpentine symbolism runs deep and has much to offer modern charmers.

Scot (1584) describes a common connection between folk-magical practitioners and the charming of serpents:

> In the citie of Salisborogh there was an
> inchanter, that before all the people tooke
> upon him to conjure all the serpents and

snakes within one mile compasse into a great pit or dike, and there to kill them. When all the serpents were gathered together, as he stood upon the brinke of the pit, there came at last a great and horrible serpent, which would not be gotten downe with all the force of his incantations: so as (all the rest being dead) he flew upon the inchanter, and clasped him in the middest, and drew him downe into the said dike, and there killed him.

While Scot uses this tale to illustrate what he considers outlandish beliefs related to the charming of serpents, he nonetheless preserves a common thread in folk practice. His work illustrates how, as he says, "poperie agreeth with paganism," which is to say that the liturgy and ritual of Catholicism facilitated the preservation of more ancient pagan practices and symbols, as in the following "popish" charm:

I conjure thee O serpent in this houre, by the five holie woonds of our Lord, that thou remove not out of this place, but here staie, as certeinelie as God was borne of a pure virgine. * Otherwise: I conjure thee serpent *In nominee patris, & filii, & spiritus sancti:*

> I command thee serpent by our ladie S.
> Marie, that thou obeie me, as wax obeieth
> the fier, and as fier obeieth water, that thou
> neither hurt me, nor anie other Christian, as
> certeinelie as God was borne of an
> immaculate virgine, in which respect I take
> thee up, *In nominee patris & filii, & spiritus*
> *sancti: Ely lash eiter, ely lash eiter, ely lash*
> *eiter.*

Charm-work involving serpents survived and thrived also in the new world, where among many others, a charm for conjuring rain still exists, recorded in folkloric "superstitious" texts like Thomas & Thomas' (1920) *Kentucky Superstitions:*

> ...If a snake crosses your path, there will be
> rain.
> ...To kill a snake and turn it over will cause
> rain.
> ...If a black snake is killed and hung on a
> fence, rain will come.
> ...The hanging of a black snake up by the
> tail will bring rain before night.

We must understand here that the charming and conjuring of serpents, the compulsion of their will by the will of the magician, is a sorcerous act parallel to the conjuration of the Devil and his demons. By the early modern period, Christians had already established that the serpent in the Garden of Eden was to be interpreted by parishioners as Satan himself, but they only arrived at this interpretation after centuries of pagan symbolism and serpent imagery. The choice to connect the serpent of old with the emerging, rapidly cementing concept of the Christian Devil only further augmented the Devil's nature as a repository for older pagan spiritual concepts.

In fact, the popular folk tale of St. Patrick driving all the snakes out of Ireland is a symbolic one, referring instead to his victory (or seeming victory) over paganism. Ancient pagan imagery in Ireland is teeming with serpents, as scholarship has long attested:

> The singular cross of Killamery, Kilkeny Co., exhibits thereon two Irish serpents. The font of Cashel illustrates the same mystery. The writer saw several stones at Cashel cathedral with sculptured snakes,

one large specimen ornamenting a sarcophagus. The Crozier, or Pastoral Staff of Cashel, which was found last century, bears a serpent springing out of a sheath or vagina. The end of the sheath is adorned with wreathing serpents. In the handle a man stands on a serpent's head with a staff, at which the reptile bites. The staff was like that of a Roman augur, or of an Etruscan and Babylonian priest.

Brash's *Sculptured Crosses of Ireland* refers to one cross, at Clonmel, having four serpents at the centre, coiled around a spherical boss. Several instances were known in which the serpents have been more or less chipped away from off such crosses.

A serpent occupies a large space on the beautiful Irish sculptured stone, *Clwyn Macnos*, or Clon Macnois. Not long ago, a stone serpent was discovered, with twelve divisions, marked as for the twelve astronomical signs, reminding one of the Babylonian serpent encircling the zodiac. Several ancient Irish fonts have upon them sculptured serpents. Glass snakes of various colours have also been frequently turned up... (Bonwick, 1894)

Clearly, St. Patrick did *not* drive all the snakes from Ireland, for like other Celtic cultures, the ancient serpent imagery that survives there is pagan in origin and is deeply knit with lore and ancestry, into the stories and songs and art itself, woven so deeply therein that it can never be truly removed.

In trying to understand the importance of the serpent to our pagan ancestors, we should consider here the popular folk-tale theme of the "white serpent," a motif that is incredibly well-catalogued in folkloric studies because it is present in so many older stories across the world.

This folk tale presents itself in the Grimm collection with the simple title of "The White Snake." In this tale, a very wise king has the mysterious power of knowing all the secrets in his kingdom. His servant brings him a dish each knight which he eats in secrecy. One evening, the servant peeks at the covered dish to discover the body of a white serpent, and he is unable to resist the temptation to taste of it. He then discovers that the flesh of the white serpent grants the power to understand animal voices, to discern the language of all living things. Through this power, the servant befriends a series of animal spirits and accomplishes a variety of tasks laid out before him, eventually discovering the golden apple of the Tree of Life, which allows him to marry the princess and ascend in station. It is, on the one hand, a tale about a protagonist who aids a variety of creatures along his journey, and is then rewarded with supernatural aid in the accomplishment of his quest. On the other hand, it is a tale containing mysteries, stressing the value of listening to and understanding the spirits of other, non-human creatures in the world, and emphasizing the spiritual aid they can provide. It echoes themes in the biblical story of Eden, but in a different light, focusing on the value of hidden knowledge and the ability of the "serpent" to awaken understanding.

More curious still is the evolution of the "white serpent" theme from its ancient roots, for it is so utterly similar to the "salmon of knowledge" from Celtic myth that one cannot ignore the parallels. This similarity is likely due to an early mingling of Norse and Gaelic cultures. In Irish myth, the salmon of knowledge is featured in a variety of texts, including the *Fintan mac Bochra*, the *Tuan mac Cairill*, and recountings of the adventures of *Fionn mac Cumhaill*. The

salmon is a primordial being that once dwelt in
an ancient well of wisdom beneath a sacred hazel
tree. Nine hazelnuts fell from that tree into the
well, and as the salmon ate them, its body
absorbed all the wisdom of the world. Fionn, in
different iterations of this tale, consumes part or
all of the salmon, thereby becoming wise for the
rest of his life. The Welsh Taliesin appears to be
a cousin to this tale, for he, too, gains wisdom by
consuming a mysterious substance, this time from
the cauldron of Cerridwen.

For ancient peoples, serpents and sea-life were
believed to be connected, forms of the same living
family of beings, and so it is no wonder that the
form of the serpent traipses into the salmon. In
fact, the idea of an ancient and primodial sea-
serpent pre-existing creation is well-attested in
myth. In the *Enuma Elish*, we find Tiamat,
described as a monstrous female serpent, whose
body is made up of all the waters of the world, a
symbol of primordial chaos before creation. It is
only after Marduk slays her that her serpentine
flesh is divided into Heaven and earth, thus laying
the foundations of the world.

Figure 32. A pair of witches conjure from their cauldron.
Adapted from *The Devil in Britain and America* (1896).

This ancient serpent, too, it seems, contained within her all things. If this story of dividing "Heaven and earth" out of a primordial body of chaos sounds familiar, reader, you may note a later form of this story, adapted by the Hebrews into the creation myth found in Genesis: "And God made the firmament, and divided the waters which were under the firmament from the waters which were above the firmament: and it was so." The origin of the primordial "waters" in this passage actually stems from the ancient serpent whose body contained all things.

By following this thread of lore, we see at last perhaps part of the reason surviving folk magics suggest using the body of the serpent to conjure waters from the sky. The serpent is both a primordial being connected with the waters of life and a symbol of that which encompasses us, its body containing all things in creation, encircling the universe itself, including older concepts of the watery "firmament" believed once to surround the earth. The serpent's wisdom is not simply the wisdom to understand the individual facets of creation, but is in fact the symbol of creation itself, of life, and of all the things that exist. Perhaps, on some deep and unconscious level, this is why the authors of the Solomonic grimoires such as the *Clavicula Salomonis* depict a serpent encompassing its magical circles, coiled about the practitioner, an echo of the ancient glyph of the ouroboros, the alchemical serpent swallowing its own tail, formed in a perfect circle.

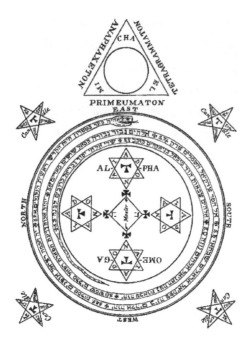

Figure 33. Magic circle featuring serpent. Adapted
from the *Clavicula Salomonis* (1400s).

Perhaps this is also somehow, on some deeply
ingrained human cognitive level, related to the
prominent Nordic mythic pattern of the serpent-
about-the-world, the Jormungandr, a great sea
snake of such size that it encircles the world and
grasps its own tail.

Yet it is in our own night sky that we find
some of the oldest lore attached to the primordial

serpent. The constellation Draco, which simply means *dragon*, is visible throughout the year from the northern hemisphere, its length coiling across its fourteen stars. The star Thuban, which belongs to this constellation, was at one time the pole star of the North, recognized by ancient Egyptian and Greek astrologers for many ages. The mythic origins of this constellation are mainly Greek, but vary depending on the teller in ancient mythic texts, ranging from beings synonymous with the great "Python" slain by Apollo to one of the gigantes slain by Athena. In each case, though, Draco is depicted as aligned with an older set of powers preceding the Olympian gods, an ancient authority that would have been associated with the watery chaos before creation.

It is unsurprising, then, that "dragon" becomes synonymous with "Satan" in the course of the church's development across the world. These myths and tales related to an ancient serpent somehow tied to creation itself contained pagan wisdom, and like so many other elements of surviving lore, became bound up in our Devil as well.

Figure 34. Devil as dragon. Adapted from
The Devil in Britain and America (1896).

A more basic question is this: why was the serpent
itself so important to so many ancient cultures?
What is it about the nature of the serpent that
suggested knowledge, secrecy, and something
fundamental to the nature of creation, to the fabric
of life itself? Part of the answer here may lie in
the behavior of snakes. Like amphibians, the
serpent has evolved to dwell in all places: on the
earth, in trees, in waters, and even underground.
The passage of the serpent between these
kingdoms still to this day speaks to us, perhaps
especially to witches, for we understand more than
most the value of the power to cross between
realms. The fact that the serpent can burrow
beneath ground, into the realm of the dead, signals

its chthonic nature, while its ability to shed its skin and renew itself reveals its potent vitality. The serpent itself, as a creature, encompasses within it these easily recognizable symbols of sovereignty, of cyclical movement from life to death to rebirth, and its sometimes venomous nature speaks to the potency we seek in our magics.

Francis Barrett (1801) suggests a very similar interpretation of the serpent's inherent symbolism in *The Magus*, a grimoire well-circulated among cunning folk and other folk-magical practitioners:

> ...for the Egyptians and Phoenicians do extol this creature above all others, and say it is a divine creature, and hath a divine nature; for in this is a more acute spirit, and a greater fire than in any other, which thing is manifest both by his swift motion without feet, hands, or any other instruments; and also that it often renews its age with his skin, and becomes young again...

If our Devil is, in part, the primordial serpent of lore, then we must be ready to face a certain set of questions. What does it mean, in the old lore and myth, that the serpent's body is supposed

to contain the primordial ingredients for creation
and awakening? What does it mean that this being
is so often subdued, divided, or consumed in order
to spark transformation (both of the earth and the
mind)? Given how often this pattern of lore
repeats, we should consider that perhaps the
serpent's death and consumption is not necessarily
the victory of one god over another. Perhaps the
serpent is *meant* to come apart, that its purpose
is to engage the story at exactly that moment
where chaos and destruction give way to order and
creation. Perhaps the nature of our Serpent of the
Abyss is not simply antagonistic, but cathartic, a
force that quickens progress in the cycle of life,
death, and renewal. The old myths paint only a
vague picture of the universe before order and
structure is imposed upon it. The world of the
Greek Titans was raw and inhospitable; the watery
abyss before creation was full of chaos. It is the
nature of all things to come apart, to degrade;
disease, aging, and death are largely the result of
this slow and necessary decay from inherent
cellular structures into what we might call chaos.
It is the serpent that symbolically facilitates the
release of chaos, the death of the old and decayed

world, into a new order, into a renewal that brings life. In this way, even the serpent's destructive powers are purposeful and life-giving. The Serpent of the Abyss does not actually die, but merely sheds its skin, its body emerging from itself, taking the form of the new that is to come. The wisdom of the serpent is not tied to its destruction, but to the ability of life to pass from one form to another. What does it mean, after all, to become wise? We might say, at a basic level, it is to outgrow one's older understanding, to shed the the worldview of our old ignorance—to become, in some ways, new.

Figure 35. A witch meets her familiar spirit, a gift from the Man in Black. Adapted from *The History of Witches and Wizards* (1720).

Conclusion:
"In the Devil's Name"

In the infamous testimony of Isobel
Gowdie, a Scottish witch from the
1600s, we find a key phrase that emerges
in nearly all of the verbal charms she provides: "in
the Devil's name" (Wilby, 2010). In Isobel's tales,
given without any evidence of torture or
compulsion, she describes flying in the Devil's
name, cursing victims in the Devil's name, and
even shifting her own form into a hare, a cat, and
a crow in the Devil's name. The Devil is, in her
account, a frightening figure, but he is also without
any doubt a source of power in her art, ultimately
similar to the priests she had probably witnessed
many times conducting their own magical rites in

the name of the Father, Son, and Holy Spirit. Nor is her description of charming in the Devil's name unique; we find iterations of this manner of incantation virtually everywhere that witches were described in early-modern lore, like the Basque witches, quite a bit more than a stone's throw from Scotland, who were said to proclaim "va au nom du Diable."

Names hold power. It is in the act of naming that we give form to the unfamiliar, create something knowable out of that which is unknown. It is with names that we call to others, signaling that we recognize them, and that they are not strangers to us. A child who is named is suddenly made real. It is no longer simply an infant, but a person. The grimoires of old and the folk-magical practices of today are full of names, some known and some secret. Verbal magical formulae are no longer shrouded in secret, but are published openly, their forms in plain sight, their true power available only to those with the wisdom to utilize them correctly. Likewise, the names of spirits are now well-disseminated, though few have the skills to utilize them without harming themselves in the process. Even today, though, there exist secret names, ways of knowing and calling to the otherworld and to our Devil that are more private, more privileged, signifying a more personal relationship with the dweller across the gate. In our present information age, I believe it is these names that now retain the most potency.

But here is the snag: our Devil's nature is not singular, but pluralistic, encompassing many different titles and meanings over the ages, a vast sea fed by so many rivers. And our access to him is fraught with dangers and barriers, for so many cultures have, over time, treated him as a repository for "dangerous" ideas, remnants of paganism and animist spirituality that frustrated the church. To discuss our Devil's many natures is one thing, but to actually call to him is another. We must know, in some way, to *whom* we are calling. Otherwise, we are merely doing the spiritual equivalent of shouting "Hey, you" across a room full of people. We must not only have a clear picture of the entity to whom we are speaking, but must make the call as if we fully *expect an answer.* How many sorcerers have attempted to intone magical names over the ages only to find themselves standing alone like a fool in a candlelit room? We are not, in the act of calling to an ancient spirit, merely pronouncing words to the air around us; we are speaking to an other who is known, to a hidden someone. Many believe that the spirits we call to are in some ways hidden parts of ourselves, and this is partially true, but *we must know that they are real, listening, and ready to answer.* Otherwise, there's no point in calling to them at all.

As I've said before, dear reader, some books are more than books. If you have taken your time and read this work carefully, you may have some sense of what I speak already. Perhaps you have felt someone following along with you as you made your way through this book. Perhaps you have had odd dreams or daydreams in which you encountered a stranger, someone you've never met who nonetheless seems vaguely familiar, like a distant relative or lost acquaintance. You may have felt that this is someone you once knew, and yet, someone new. A familiar stranger. A faceless beloved. Perhaps you merely felt the sensation of *not being alone*, the instinctive sense of being in another person's presence. By now, you no doubt understand: this book is designed, in part, to affect a magical unbinding, not because it contains within it some hidden, unconscious formula, but because, through the course of these pages, we have examined carefully individual aspects of a being most of us have spent our lives locking away, avoiding, or ignoring. In order to arrive at this juncture, which is, make no mistake, a gate standing before us, waiting to be opened, it was necessary to first come to know some of the aspects we refer to when we say "the Devil." After all, *we can only call out to those we know.*

If the prospect of opening this gate frightens you, that's okay. You can close this book. You can shelve it. You can set it aside somewhere and never open it again. This path isn't right for everyone, and the dangers of calling to dark entities are very real. Many people are raised in such oppressively religious households that there is real trauma bound up in the idea of "the Devil." For some of these people, opening this gate means facing decades of pain and abuse. Turning away from this kind of door is not cowardly, but often wise if we are unprepared to face what lies on the other side. Make no mistake, though—*the only horror waiting there is that of our own design.*

This is the true nature of the curse we have set out to break. It is a binding we have placed on the most shunned and hated parts of our human selves: our animal selves, our shameless selves, our pre-Christian selves, our pre-civilization selves, our sorcerous selves, our antiauthoritarian selves, our marginalized selves, our othered selves, forgotten and objectified, bound like demons we thought we could exorcise, but somehow never forgotten or destroyed, just waiting there, beyond the threshold, a stranger watching in the dark.

For witches, calling to the Devil is an act of resistance, empowerment, and affirmation. We are not merely calling to a generic "father god" or "horned god," but to the very Devil of myth and lore, to the ancestor of the witches' line, the First Sorcerer, the shamanic magus depicted in cave paintings, to the Chief of Spirits, Founder of the Hosts of Faery, to the Beast-Lord of the Sabbat, uniting the human and animal realms, to the Spirit in the Green, the spirit of the land who rises and falls with the crops, to the indwelling spirit of flora, to the Serpent of the Abyss, the very embodiment of natural cycles of decay and renewal. When we call to the Devil, we align ourselves with one or more of these or other aspects of his nature, drawing power from that potent place where fear and desire are mingled. We are calling to our parent and to our power. We are calling to a spiritual inheritance, a birthright rescued from obscurity. He is not simply *the* Devil, but *our* Devil, a spiritual pattern after which we instinctively follow. This reveals that we are somehow also kin to the entities we conjure, that our souls are in a sense knit from the same material, that when we summon the spirit forth, we are in some ways calling to some hidden part of ourselves. These keys empower us in unique ways as witches, for we are not some power-hungry wish-makers exhausting our energy as we try to compel the genie to appear, but are instead magical beings ourselves, calling to our very own long-lost kin, flexing a muscle that has simply lain dormant. Our work in spirit conjuration is not merely the achievement of desires (though it can include this), but a sacred unbinding, a restoration of the bonds between living witches and our otherworldly brethren. It is the unleashing of power, conducted safely and carefully, with reverence and caution. The truth is that we need not force the spirit to arrive, only permit it to do so, for we are witches, and the beloved has been with us all along.

In this act, we reject the voices of religious authorities who have, over the years, stripped us of our folk traditions, which is to say, the traditions of the people, and we align ourselves with those forgotten and abused spirits in the deep who are, in fact, descended from our first spiritual allies, our oldest teachers and guides. We do this for much the same reason we call ourselves "witches" in the first place, despite the negative connotations bound up in this term. It is, in the end, *an act of love*, a deep empathy with those who have been hated and shunned for their magical inclinations over the ages, and an equal empathy for those spirits who were once the gods of conquered peoples, commanded and constrained under new, self-proclaimed "masters."

Do not mistake this affirmative act for a safe one. We are not calling to a being of "love and light," but to a spirit of a complex and mingled nature, at times as cruel and cunning as we ourselves can be. We are calling to shadow, which is a dangerous art, for it requires that we know and master the shadow within ourselves. In some ways, calling to the Devil is a kind of spiritual test. If we have shed the fear and shame that holds together our preconceived notions about dark spirits, then we may meet success. If we know and accept our own darkness, embracing it as a necessary and useful part of our own selves, then we may stand in its presence without losing our footing. On the other hand, if we still carry shame at our dark selves and worship at the altar of some fictive ideal of "purity," then calling to the Devil brings great danger, for we are merely another generation of oppressors calling to the spirits we have abused for so many ages. Kindling cannot approach the flame; to make the journey, we must be stone.

Calling to our Devil, like any form of spirit conjuration, requires that the witch has already mastered what we call "witch-sight," or the ability to perceive spiritual currents and beings, a curriculum of art that eventually culminates in the craft of leaving the physical body in order to venture in into the otherworld directly. I have written extensively about these methods in my previous book, *A Broom at Midnight*, but I will provide a brief overview here as well. Essentially, the witch must "loosen" the spirit from the body to affect an altered consciousness, and this can be done in many ways. I recommend beginning simply with a single lit candle in a dark room, moving the hands before the candle's flame so as to create shadows that pass over the eyelids. This repetitive movement of shadow and light, though simple, has a distinct effect on the witch's consciousness. It creates a lulling rhythm out of fluctuating degrees of darkness, and this rhythm often gives way to swaying, heavy breathing, and a sense of release that is difficult to describe. Psychologists would call this a form of autohypnosis, but its methodology is ancient, predating the existence of science itself. Awakening one's spiritual senses is, in fact, an act of magic.

The more focused methods of *Via Repetitio, Via Veneficium, Via Imaginibus,* and *Via Umbrum* are all equally useful in this work. These, along with nine other methods, are discussed more fully in my previous work. The first of these pertains to the use of repeated actions and incantations, often the counting of beads upon the rosary with the fingers or the rhythmic recitation of spoken charms. *Via Veneficium* encompasses the witch's arsenal of psychoactive herbal preparations, including nightshades, artemisias, alcohol, cannabis, and many others. I recommend the use of a good mugwort ointment for this purpose, as it is both very effective and generally safer than nightshade preparations, which require a great deal of expertise. For obvious reasons, those who are pregnant or have existing medical conditions should perhaps consider another approach entirely. *Via Imaginibus* entails a meditative gaze upon images, including sigils and seals that represent gateways through which the spirit may pass. These can be elaborate or simple, designed by the witch upon the floor using chalk. *Via Umbrum* is perhaps the most effortless, for it relies on the dark itself. Extinguishing the candle and submersing oneself in darkness will awaken the otherworldly senses quite effectively, though the intensity of the visions that follow can be startling for those unprepared.

In conjunction with one or more of these methods, it is possible to call to the Devil plainly, as the witches of old have done, following the pattern of conjurations preserved in our lore.

Rather than calling him as the biblical Satan, which is perhaps the most limiting way of approaching this spirit, we may call him as *Antecessor, Man in Black, Eman Hetan, Dominus Umbrarum, Robinus Filius Artis, Benedicite, Primus Magus, Elva, Hamerlin, Peterlin, Kochloffel, Janicot, Jaune, Azazel, Lucifer Who Turns the Wheel, Puca Geal, Puca Dubh, Hob Who Keeps the Lantern, Walliman, Black and Comely Magister, Serpent of the Deep, Worm of Pale Flesh, Barrabon, King of Elphame, Founder of Faery, Beast of the Sabbat, Star of the East,* and by many other names derived from our great inheritance of witch-lore. We may call him by simple means, alone at our altars in the dark, our candles lit, trusting his influence to empower our charms, to pass through us as we burn fumigations of mugwort and juniper, to attend to us in visions as we induce our ecstasies of inebriation and meditative transcendence. These forms of summoning connect us with the witches of the past, aligning our own calls with theirs, identifying us to this spirit not as isolated practitioners, but participants in a long lineage of craft. We become, in adopting these old words, the latest living witches in the procession of charmers who have called to him throughout the ages, and via this alignment, we are more likely to meet one of his aspects he intends for witches, rather than one of his less welcoming aspects reserved for those unworthy of his gifts.

It is also possible to conjure our Devil in more unique aspects via the adaptation of grimoiric formulae. Using the spirit seals as provided in the old grimoires is not something I recommend, for as we have seen, the history of calling to "demonic" deities is actually a history of spiritual violence. Instead, I recommend trying to understand a spirit's nature and altering the seal and spoken conjuration accordingly. We can read the old grimoiric operations as examples of how an enemy would call to this spirit. How, then, would we do so as an ally? How would we do so as a friend? We can rely on divination and visionary experiences to guide us in this craft, to provide us with the right adjustments to the old formulae. In effect, we are adjusting the radio dial and calling to a different aspect of this spirit. This does not mean we should abandon the use of magical protection and defense. Instead of shouting, "Hey, you—hideous, hated thing who deserves to be tormented, get over here or I'll hurt you," we are saying, "Spirit, you are welcome here. I will not harm you, and you will not harm me, for we are kin. Come." It is often recommended to conduct this work with the inclusion of conjurations to deities, ancestors, saints, or other spirits who can gently guide the entity over and ensure that no harm is exchanged in the process—either to you or to them.

The spirit perceived in the act of calling to the Devil must be understood in the context of the pluralistic, myriad being that he is, as attested in our lore. His nature will appear differently from one witch to another, and it will also vary in one witch's experience over time. We have learned from so many currents of lore that our Devil assumes forms relevant to one's heritage, one's culture, and one's landscape. Even the witch's familiar or imp is often discussed in the lore as a representative of his spirit. As is often the case in witchcraft, we must resist overcomplicating what our senses tell us. Effective craft is grounded in instinct.

As our Devil's aspects are slowly unveiled to the witch, we become empowered with knowledge, and are able to utilize names and seals to lend great potency to our workings. The great number of *in nominee* formulae found in our lore are really a testament to the syncretic and heretical magics that are such a vital part of folk witchcraft. Once we know and understand an aspect of our Devil, we can charge magical acts in its name. These names are often personal, and as such, it is not recommended that they be shared with other practitioners unless the spirit explicitly permits you to do so, which is a rare event, for names hold power, and a spiritual name revealed to the witch is a great act of trust.

You have certainly inferred by now, dear reader, that calling to the witches' Devil is not, in the grand sense, a singular event, but an iterative process, not a sudden encounter, but a slow arrival. His nature is revealed incrementally as we approach individual aspects of his being over the course of years. The labor of witches, and the nature of initiation itself, does not actually end. There is no real point at which the witch can say she has "arrived," that her work is actually "done."

As we call to this ancient spirit, we are slowly unwinding a spool, and we are growing in wisdom and in power, but the length of yarn we draw ever replenishes itself. We forever seek a realization of our originator, of our teacher and guide, that is more and more vivid, more potent, more fully formed. We call to our Devil not with the assumption that he will ever cross a final threshold, but with the hope that our eyes become slowly opened to his nature, that we grow more attuned, and that our craft, grounded in the lore of the past, ever reaches towards that next, more accomplished gate that we would hope to cross. The attainment of a perfect and unchanging craft is an illusion. We are, like our Devil, creatures that ever escape boundaries, ever yearning and reaching.

Like a pair of beloveds, the witch and the Devil seek one another in the dark, over and over, an eternal dance, and their precious moments of contact can never fully sate the desire for that communion. That longing for the other is knit within us. The beloved is always there, waiting, just beyond the bend, calling out to us in the dark. What path will carry us to his sabbat this night?

What woodland trail, what midnight bridge will bring us to his grove?

Figure 36. A warlock meets with his Devil. Adapted from
The History of Witches and Wizards (1720).

Carmina Magistra*

I.

Sweet is the song that calls my beloved.
Long and winding is the crown upon his head.

I have come to the black meadow at midnight
To sound my call upon the cold night air.

Thrice have I dreamt of my beloved's voice
Carried from the hill that is the grave.

Thrice have I worn his chill breath upon me
Into the sun-lit world of men and beasts.

---

* Songs of the Magister, or Teacher. These mystery songs
are offered here as fable, riddle, and incantation, patterned
after the Devil's aspect as Rex Aenigmatus or King of
Riddles. Though original, their imagery and contents are
lore-sourced and reflect a continuation of the traditions of
both pagan hymn and subversive psalmistry.

Thrice have I purged all promises made
That would bind my spirit from his touch.

The seed is wet and black and strong
In its furrow, reaching from its mound

For the light of the star he carries,
For the beating heart of the hind.

II.

I met my beloved in a churchyard.
Black and comely was his dress.

He gave to me a name I keep in secret,
Written upon a rib bone hidden.

He cradled me from head to foot
And kindled all between his hands.

The blood of my heart he called sweet.
The flesh of my body he called lovely.

My scars he set as jewels in silver,
The bindings upon my hands as bangles.

I raised my voice like a newborn crying out
As he lit my candle from his ember crown.

III.

I walked with my beloved to the crossroads,
The juncture at which all things may meet.

In the North, I saw the towering tree;
In the Northeast, a field swaying with grain;

In the Southeast, a corpse holding a lantern;
In the South, a procession over the snow;

In the Southwest, a great number of candles;
In the Northwest, a great swelling of flame.

My beloved stood at the center of three roads
And held out a star in his fearsome hand.

Six paths fix all things in space, he said.
Six are the directions of arriving and going.

Three are the lines of the crossroads, he said,
Three in one, all paths conjoined:

The living, the dreaming, and the dead.
For lack of one, there be none.

IV.

My beloved is a king with many subjects.
Nine are the oldest to accompany him

Upon the tides of the deep. Nine teachers
And nine guides to pass the flame to the people,

Carried on breath and word and sign
That our craft may never be truly lost.

Azazel first, whose forge is our cunning
And whose fires illuminate the way.

Semjaza, who keeps the measure of every
Leaf and root for our conjurations.

Armaros, who bends enchantments back
Upon themselves like the cracking branch.

Baraqijal, who teaches the secrets of the stars
And the light they cast upon the darkness.

Kokabel, who weaves between the stars
To preserve their signs for the people.

Ezeqeel, whose voice calls wind and cloud,
Stirring the sky with his long arm.

Araqiel, who reaches deep within the earth
To wrest secrets from that dark kingdom.

Shamsiel, who plots the course of blazing sun
Across the seasons of all things.

Sariel, adrift in the wake of the moon,
Who knows the secrets of that lamp.

Nine spirits cunning, nine spirits guiding,
To answer the call of the people.

V.

My beloved was born in the cool of spring,
His bones buried deep in the valley.

His horns erupted into bright blooms,
His tears as snowdrops in the green.

My beloved towered over the field
At the height of summer, his beard unfolding.

His eyes were gold and sweet as honey.
His belly hung like a generous peach.

My beloved was slaughtered in the autumn.
His blood kissed every swaying grain.

His coat shifted in the cold wind
as a silvered field beset with breeze.

My beloved was buried in the winter,
His flesh as cold and still as stone.

Beneath the grave his heart beat yet
As a wild music, as hooves upon the deep.

VI.

Black is the color of my beloved.
Black as night sky, black as the unseen keeps

Beneath the earth. His pulpit is the briar hedge
Dividing kingdom from kingdom;

His gospel is the road between the roads;
His hymnal is the breath we take between

The prayers of every faith. Black are his eyes,
Black his tongue. Black as the perfect silence

In the hush before and after every sermon;
Black as the beauty of dark waters.

VII.

Two-headed is my beloved, who stands sentinel
At the gate. His gaze is soft and terrible,

Witness to seen and unseen kingdoms,
To all gone before and all yet to be,

To all comings and all goings,
All kindness and all cruelty.

Any who cross his threshold dire
Must meet his eyes and answer his riddle.

His dreaming gate is hewn of wood
Cut from a tree that never grew.

VIII.

My beloved is like a cup of spirits
That quickens ecstasy through the veins.

My beloved is like the blue-gray smoke
That brings great pleasure to the mind.

My beloved is like the nightshade plucked
To heal or to ruin all flesh. His venom

Is the pleasure and delight of all peoples,
And his sacrament is the rapturous cry

Of the mind blooming within itself,
The spirit shaking loose from its husk,

Like the seed that rattles from its pod,
Like the fruit that swells from shriveled petals.

IX.

My beloved's court lies under the hill,
Among a secret and hidden people.

My beloved's queen is a comely lady
Who holds her feasts in the cool of graves.

My beloved's subjects are infinite as stars,
Wandering from their cities deep

On unseen roads in sojourn, all joy and fury,
To bless and to curse by fate's decree.

As once he fell, streaming through the night,
So did his people journey with him,

To craft within the earth such palaces
Worthy to guard the secrets he keeps.

X.

The light of my beloved's crown
Is starlight, sunlight, and moonlight all.

Its flame is passed unto the people
That they may see to work in the dark,

An inheritance shared with those who seek him
In the furthest reaches of the night.

My beloved's light is a star transfixed
Between his terrible antlers,

A jewel plucked from the stars of Heaven,
Carried to the earth like rain.

His candle is the lantern set in welcome
Upon black nights, to hint the path.

XI.

My beloved is the first of masters,
The greatest and first of sorcerers all.

A-hunting goes my beloved in the glade,
Seeking the soul with his smooth darts.

My beloved is like the serpent winding
Through the leaves and detritus underfoot,

His white scales glimmering in the moonlight
are like a stream of milk through the moss.

He knows the breathing of every creature.
No sound or footprint can escape his knowing.

My beloved's campfire is veiled in shadows.
All pupils of craft seek its glow and smolder.

In the thick of the forest, his embers gleam
Between the hanging bones and skins of prey.

With his tools, he bends the shape of all things
And teaches the arts of bending even the soul.

XII.

Father and mother is my beloved,
Wise teacher of all craft that is hidden.

His tutelage sows strength in weakness,
Wisdom even in wild innocence.

My beloved teaches the likeness of things,
To craft the simulacra of art that catches

The soul, that we may charm it.
My beloved teaches the movement of power,

That it flows like contagion towards the enemy.
My beloved teaches how to call

Unto the indwelling spirit of all things,
To forge agreements and pacts to hold

The visible and invisible in harmony.
My beloved teaches the natures of plants,

Roots, herbs, stones, and bones of beasts,
To discern what power each may hold

For harm or aid. My beloved teaches
The oscillation of signs, to cast or to read

The workings of sortilege, the churning stars,
The undulations of water and flame

To divine the truth beneath what is seen.
My beloved teaches the ecstasy of the soul,

The sending of the spirit beyond the body,
To seek out knowledge through hidden doors.

XIII.

O beloved whose name is the moonlit dark,
O beloved redder than the day,

O beloved whose name is a tuneless dance,
O beloved louder than the pipe,

O beloved whose name is a stitchless shirt,
O beloved sharper than the thorn,

O beloved whose name is a waterless stream,
O beloved deeper than the sea,

O beloved whose name is a stepless stair,
O beloved longer than the way,

Antecessor, come and carry me.
I have nothing which is not thine.

Bibliography

Allies, J. (1852). *On the Ancient British, Roman, and Saxon Antiquities and Folk-lore of Worcestershire.* J. H. Parker.

Barrett, F. (1801). *The Magus, or Celestial Intelligencer; Being a Complete System of Occult Philosophy.* Lackington, Allen, and Co.

Bonwick, J. (1894). *Irish Druids and Old Irish Religions.* Griffith, Farran.

Burns, R. (1897). "Tam Lin." In A. Lang, *A Collection of Ballads.* Chapman and Hall.

Burton, John Hill. (1852). *Narratives from Criminal Trials in Scotland (vol. 2).* Chapman and Hall.

Carod-Artal, F. J. (2013). Psychoactive Plants in Ancient Greece. *Neurosciences and History, 1* (1): 28-38.

Corbeill, A. (2009) "Weeping Statues, Weeping Gods, and Prodigies from Republican to

Early-Christian Rome." *Tears in the Greco-Roman World*. Fogen.

Crowley, A. (1995). *The Goetia: The Lesser Key of Solomon the King*. Samuel Weiser.

Davis, H. J. (1975). *The Silver Bullet, and Other American Witch Stories*. Jonathan David Publishers.

Day, J. (2010). *Yahweh and the Gods and Goddesses of Canaan*. Bloomsbury.

Evans-Wentz, W. Y. (1911). *The Fairy-Faith in Celtic Countries*. Oxford University Press.

Folkard, R. (1884). *Plant Lore, Legends, and Lyrics: Embracing the Myths, Traditions, Superstitions, and Folk-lore of the Plant Kingdom*. S. Low, Marston, Searle, and Rivington.

Frazer, J. G. (1890). *The Golden Bough*. Macmillan.

Gonzalez-Whippler, M. (1991). *The New Revised 6th and 7th Books of Moses and the Magical Uses of the Psalms*. Original Publications.

Grieves, M. (1931). *A Modern Herbal*. Harcourt, Brave & Company.

Guazzo, F. M. (1608). *Compendium Maleficarum.*

Heine, H. (1892). *The Works of Heinrich Heine.* Translated from the German by Charles Godfrey Leland. William Heinemann.

Huson, P. (1970). *Mastering Witchcraft.* G. P. Putnam.

Hyde, D. (1899). *A Literary History of Ireland from Earliest Times to the Present Day.* T. F. Unwin.

Jones, W. H. S., & Ormerod, H. A. (1918). *Pausanias Description of Greece with an English Translation in 4 Volumes.* Harvard University Press.

Lang, A. (1888). In *Perrault's Popular Tales.* Clarendon Press.

Le Grand Grimoire; ou l'art de commander les esprits célestes, aériens, terrestres, infernaux; avec le vrai secret de faire parler les morts, de gagner toutes les fois qu'on met aux loteries, etc. (1845)

Leland, C. G. (1899). *Aradia, or, The Gospel of the Witches.* D. Nutt.

Linton, E. L. (1861). *Witch Stories.* University of Michigan.

Lurker, M. (1987). *The Routledge Dictionary of Gods and Goddesses, Devils and Demons.* Routledge.

Mather, C. (1862). *The Wonders of the Invisible World: Being an Account of the Tryals of Several Witches Lately Executed in New England.* John Russell Smith.

Mathers, S. L. M. (1889). *The Key of Solomon the King: Clavicula Salomonis.*

Mackenzie, G. (1699). *The Laws and Customes of Scotland in Matters Criminal.*

Murray, M. A. (1921). *The Witch-Cult in Western Europe.* Clarendon Press.

Murray, M. A. (1931). *The God of the Witches.* Faber & Faber.

Nicolai, C. F. (1782). *Versuch über die Beschuldigungen welche dem Tempelherrenorden gemacht worden, und über dessen Geheimniss ; nebst einem Anhange über das Entstehen der Freymaurergesellschaft, von Friedrich Nicolai. Erster Theil. Zweyte verbesserte Auflage.*

Patai, R. (1973). The God Yahweh-Elohim. *American Anthropologist, 75*(4): 1181-1184.

Peterson, J. H. (2007). *Grimorium Verum.* Createspace.

Ratsch, C. (2005). *The Encyclopedia of Psychoactive Plants.* Park Street Press.

Ridenour, A., & Tejaratchi, S. (2016). *The Krampus and the Old, Dark Christmas: Roots and Rebirth of the Folkloric Devil.* Feral House.

Schultes, R. E. (1970). The plant kingdom and hallucinogens. *Bulletin on Narcotics, 22* (1). 25-53.

Scot, R. (1584). *The Discoverie of Witchcraft.*

Sidky, H. (2010). *Witchcraft, Lycanthropy, Drugs and Disease: An Anthropological Study of the European Witch-Hunts.* Wipf and Stock.

Smith, W. (1871). *A New Classical Dictionary of Greek and Roman Biography, Mythology, and Geography.* Harper & Brothers.

Thomas, L. B., & Thomas, D. L. (1920). *Kentucky Superstitions*. Princeton University Press.

Thompson, R. L. (1919). *The History of the Devil: The Horned God of the West*. Harcourt Brace.

Walsh, W. S. (1897). *Curiosities of Popular Customs and of Rites, Ceremonies, Observances, and Miscellaneous Antiquities*. Lippincott Company.

Wasson, R. G., Hoffman, A., & Puck, C. A. P. (2008). *The Road to Eleusis: Unveling the Secret of the Mysteries*. North Atlantic Books.

Wilby, E. (2010). *The Visions of Isobel Gowdie: Magic, Witchcraft, and Dark Shamanism in Seventeenth-century Scotland*. Sussex Academic Press.

Yeats, W. B. (1888). *Fairy and Folk Tales of the Irish Peasantry*. W. Scott.

About the Author

Roger J. Horne is a writer, folk witch, and modern animist. He is the author of *Folk Witchcraft, A Broom at Midnight,* and *The Witch's Art of Incantation.* His spiritual practice is informed by his ancestral currents of Scottish cunning craft and Appalachian herb-doctoring. Read more about him at rogerjhorne.com.

Made in United States
Orlando, FL
30 June 2024

48459327R00150